EssexWorks.

·· ⸱tter quality of life

How to get
a job in a
recession

Harry Freedman PhD is the Founder and Chief Executive of Career Energy, one of the most popular careers consultancies in Britain. Harry has a broad career background having worked at senior level across many sectors, including hospitality, technology, healthcare and not-for-profit. His interest in helping people to develop their careers stemmed from his own experience in making frequent career changes. He found that by identifying his dominant skills, interests and values he could identify new contexts and directions for himself and when he founded Career Energy, these techniques became the core principles behind the company's work.

HOW TO GET A JOB

IN A
RECESSION

HARRY FREEDMAN

infiniteideas

Essex County
Council Libraries

First published in 2009 by
Infinite Ideas Limited
36 St Giles
Oxford, OX1 3LD
United Kingdom
www.infideas.com

A CIP catalogue record for this book is available from the British Library

ISBN 978–1–906821–09–8

Brand and product names are trademarks or registered trademarks of their respective owners.

Cover and text designed and typeset by Baseline Arts Ltd, Oxford
Printed and bound by TJ International, Cornwall

Contents

Introduction: What is different about job hunting in a recession?   7

Finding a job

1. Where to look when nothing is being advertised   14
2. Personal networking   19
3. Online networking   29

Applying for a job

4. Understanding what you offer   38
5. Responding to job advertisements   58
6. Writing an effective CV   65
7. Making best use of recruitment consultants   90
8. Making speculative approaches 1 – doing your research   102
9. Making speculative approaches 2 – writing speculative letters   106
10. Cold calling   112
11. Application forms   120
12. Interviewing   131
13. The job offer   149

Can't get or don't want a job?

14. What are you going to do now?   154

Further support   163
Index   165

Introduction: What is different about job hunting in a recession?

The job market

The UK job market is weakening rapidly, with the number of permanent jobs available dropping at a record rate. If you are one of the many thousands of job seekers affected by redundancy, or fearing the worst, what are you going to do? Be proactive, or freeze like a rabbit in the headlights?

Losing your job can be devastating. You can expect to go through a range of emotions, high and low. You will cycle through fear, anger, bafflement, acceptance, relief, even exhilaration. All of these will affect your mood. But none will get you a job.

So what will you do? Trawl through the papers every day, fire off your CV to a thousand and one online job boards, try to phone recruitment consultants – who may not answer because they are also laying off staff? That's what everybody else is doing. And look where it's getting them. Will you be like them? Or will you take a proactive approach?

When you're hit by redundancy in a recession you can't leave your job search to chance. It is essential to try to get ahead of the game and that's what this book is about. It will help you to look for jobs more successfully than everyone else, discover more vacancies that are right for you and submit applications that present you well and have an impact.

Although the number of jobs is falling, there are still plenty of new opportunities coming onto the market. On 4th December 2008 Monster reported nearly four thousand new jobs posted that day alone. So even if there are fewer jobs in your particular industry, the chances of you getting back to work quickly in another field are still high. And this book will show you how.

Encouraging signs

There is a positive aspect to this recession, one which we have not seen before. It may be because this is potentially the most severe slump since the 1920s, it may be because it is a truly global downturn, or it may be because we are becoming smarter, nicer, wiser people. But for whatever reason, there is a spirit of co-operation out there that is quite new, and very encouraging.

It started with the government's bail outs of the banks. Of course it was based on self interest – governments want and need their economies to be successful. Nevertheless, whatever your view on their policies, the fact that governments were prepared to intervene rather than leave matters to market forces, generated a good feeling. People felt that government cared, and that made us feel better. Then we started to see international co-operation between central banks, with co-ordinated reductions of interest rates and further injection of capital into the markets. Another positive, constructive step, generating more goodwill in society at large.

And then it began to come down to the individual level. Companies, finding trading conditions difficult began to discover that their suppliers were more willing than they had been in the past to wait a bit longer for payment. Families struggling to pay mortgages were given longer to pay. Local authorities said they would pay on time, HM Revenue and Customs eased up on chasing debtors. Yes, it was all the result of self interest, but it was different from all previous recessions. I should know, I have been through a few.

Now there is evidence that we are taking this co-operative ethic further. The spirit of pulling together is moving into the jobs market. With a rapidly growing number of redundancies, and the temporary collapse of many industries, many people are looking for work in new fields. If you are one of them, you will probably have started researching new sectors to find out where you fit in best, and thought about how to make new contacts, expand your networks and re-position yourself. You will need the help of others – and you will be asked to help others.

Which brings us to a topic that many people find difficult. One of the many things we will discuss in this book, which is worth flagging up immediately, is the whole question of how you are going to get out there, meet people, look for opportunities, get your name around, step outside your comfort zone. Yes, it is that dreaded word that most people shy away from: networking. There is no doubt that networking works. And there is no doubt that most people find it uncomfortable. But there are ways of dealing with it, ways in which you can start to network effectively without fear, and without going beyond the limits of your comfort. But more on that later.

The key to job hunting

There are two things that you need to get right if you want to get a new job quickly. The first is targeting the right jobs. The other is presenting yourself effectively.

Targeting jobs means being clear about what you are looking for and where you are likely to find it. There is no point in spending time or effort applying for jobs that you don't want, or are unlikely to get. Job applications take time to write. You will be better off submitting fewer, more targeted applications than dozens of hastily written irrelevant ones.

So the next section in this book will concentrate on how you find the jobs that are right for you. Bear in mind that the industry you have been working in may no longer be the best place to look. Where else will you direct your attention? What other jobs, and companies will you target? Once you have lined up your targets, it's time to turn to how you will write your job applications. At this point your job search campaign changes from seeking to selling. How will you communicate your strengths to the employers that you are targeting? What are they looking for, and what do you offer them? Part two of this book will cover the way that you communicate your strengths, both in writing and verbally, when you apply for a job.

Finally, there is the question of what you do if you really don't want any of the jobs that are realistic for you. Remember that your career is the activity you spend more of your life on than anything else, and if you don't enjoy it, you can become demotivated, disillusioned and depressed. And that is not what this book is about. So, if there are no jobs out there for you, what can you do? There are solutions, and we will look at them in part three.

About this book

This book is the product of the work that we do at Career Energy, the best known careers consultancy in Britain. We believe that everyone is entitled to, and able to have, a successful and enjoyable career. It is true that most people have not managed to find their ideal career, and would like to find something better, but that is simply because at no point in our educational system are we taught what a career really is, and how to identify the one that is right for us.

At Career Energy our clients often tell us that the career advice they received at school or college was inadequate. Many people blame their current career direction on what seemed to be snap judgements made by careers officers in their place of education.

While it is true that much careers advice at this level is poor, this is often because students and school leavers are just not ready to think about their first job, let alone their long term career goals. When you have been in education all your life, with perhaps the occasional, low paid, weekend job, it can be difficult to understand what a full time job can be like. It is hard enough for those going into higher education to decide what course to study, let alone decide on a career future. So it is not surprising that conventional careers advice is often wide of the mark; the students are just not ready for it.

The key to a successful career lies in understanding four things: what we are good at, what we enjoy, what matters to us in life and what motivates us at work. We call them:

■ Skills
■ Interests
■ Values
■ Motivators

These may sound like easy things to understand but the devil is in the detail. For example, it is not enough to know that you are interested in watching football: to see how your interest in football might affect your career choices you need to drill down and discover what it is about football that interests you. So perhaps it is the competitive aspect, the tribal alliances, appreciation of the players' athletic abilities, the history of the game or its statistics. If you can transfer the underlying reasons why you like watching into your career, you are on the way to finding a career that you like.

All good career change advice is built around using these four principles to help people become clear about the direction their career may take. Once you understand these four factors you will have the clarity and objectivity to make an informed judgment about your future career direction.

Only then can you start to plan your job search campaign. Don't underestimate the planning aspect. There is a lot more to job hunting than responding to adverts and sending your CV to databases. The art of a successful job search campaign is first to discover the best way of finding the jobs you want and then to perfect your self-marketing, your CV and interview technique so that you really stand out from the crowd and present yourself as the ideal candidate.

In this book we will guide you carefully through all these areas in turn. We are in a recession. Times are tough. Let's get started.

Finding a job

1. Where to look when nothing is being advertised

Proactive and reactive job hunting

Have you noticed how thin the job pages in the newspapers are at the moment? Try to find a newspaper from, say, September 2008 and compare the number of job ads then with the number today. That's one of the problems with recessions. They don't just create redundancies. They also dramatically reduce the number of jobs on offer.

To get the right job at any time you need to target your search well. If you don't you will spend your time chasing jobs you don't really want; and by wasting so much of your time with unproductive job applications you increase your chances of missing the few opportunities that are right for you.

Now, if targeting is essential even in a flourishing job market, it is even more essential in a recession. So before you start looking for a job take some time to think about how you are going to target jobs, and how this targeting will affect your job search plan.

There are two types of job search and unfortunately there also seem to be two types of job seeker. There is the reactive job seeker, so called because he or she reacts to opportunities that come their way. And there is the proactive job seeker, the person who makes things happen, by spotting or even creating opportunities for themselves. You don't need a book to tell you which one is more likely to get a job.

Think about how you got your last job, and about how your friends and family members got theirs. The chances are that most people you know will have found their last job through word of mouth – perhaps a promotion, or an approach by a head hunter; maybe by a friend who wanted them to come and work for him or, quite likely, through networking.

So, if in a buoyant job market, which it has been for the last few years, most jobs come through word of mouth, how much more so in a recession where there are more job seekers? In this sort of environment there is a far greater possibility that the recruiters will be able to find someone they know, or have heard of, to fill the role.

Reactive job search methods include:
- Reading newspaper job adverts
- Visiting online job boards
- Signing up for email alerts
- Registering with recruiters and agencies

All these methods are valid and we will deal with each one in turn. Reactive job search will certainly generate lots of possible jobs for you and you will be kept busy applying for them. The trouble is that in a job market where more and more people are being made redundant daily, the number of applications for each advertised job is going to be huge, and will continue to grow as the recession deepens.

This means that every time you apply for a job you have seen advertised, or that a recruiter has drawn to your attention, you will effectively be entering a lottery. Not even the most experienced and conscientious manager can guarantee to recruit the best candidate from a thousand or more CVs that cross his desk. It all becomes a matter of pot luck. You might be the lucky one. But the chances are that you won't.

Proactive job search methods are very different. They include:

■ Networking for introductions to decision makers in the company of your choice;

■ Approaching employers directly;

■ Volunteering for unpaid work experience in the expectation that your value to the company will be discovered and you will be offered a job.

Using a proactive approach to your job search increases the likelihood that you will be one of only a few applicants for a job. And the fact that you showed initiative will stand you in good stead.

So, although we would never suggest that you can afford to overlook any avenue in your job search, and yes, you do need to read the papers and trawl the online job board; nevertheless the more proactive you can be in your job search, the greater your chances of finding and getting a job quickly. Looking for a job is a full time job in itself; the better you manage your time so that you can devote as much energy as you need to proactive methods, while ensuring that you do not overlook the reactive ones, the greater your chances of success. Particularly in a tough job market.

Research

Effective targeting is one of the two essential components of your job search (the other being first class self-presentation). You cannot be proactive without targeting accurately, you won't know where to direct your efforts. To target well you need to know what companies are out there, and what you offer that they need.

This means that you need good research. Whichever industry or sector you are seeking to work in, whether a private company, public body or voluntary organisation, you need to know who the main players are, what is happening in their business or activity at the moment, what weaknesses they have, which you will be able to strengthen, and who their key decision makers are.

A multitasked approach

Once you know all this, and have a list of the various decision makers and their contact details, all you have to do is work out how to get in front of them! This will not be as hard as it seems. We will look at research in more detail shortly but at this stage it is important to emphasise that while a book can only deal with one topic at a time, a successful job search requires you to carry out many activities simultaneously.

For example, we won't get round to discussing your CV until chapter 6 but you may need to show prospective networking contacts a CV before they agree to meet you, and we discuss networking in chapters 2 and 3. On the other hand you are likely to need to do some networking (chapters 2 and 3) before you can be clear about what a particular target company's need is, and be able to make a well focused, speculative approach to them (chapters 8 and 9).

So don't treat your job search as a straight line process, in which you finish one task before you start another. If you are going to find a job in a recession when nobody else can, you will need to be imaginative, creative, flexible and adaptable. You will have to start to multitask – it's a good discipline anyway.

The chart below shows the four main recruitment strategies, and the chances of getting a job using them. It is grouped into direct and indirect approaches, and proactive and reactive methods.

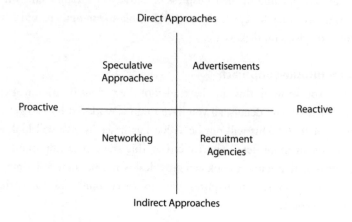

Most people only search amongst jobs that have already been advertised or given to a recruitment consultant. Their job search is reactive.

2. Personal networking

Where does networking fit into the job search strategy?

Three of our clients announced last week that they had found jobs, and two more had lined up interviews. We are in the middle of an economic downturn and unemployment is rising, so how did they do it?

In every case the opportunity arose because someone – a friend, a colleague, a networking contact, had drawn their attention to an opportunity which they felt was right for them. In one case the contact was virtual, they had never met but had connected through an online networking site. The point is that all these jobs and interviews came about through networking; a process about which many people feel uncertain, but which in an economy such as this assumes even more importance.

There is little doubt that networking is the most effective method for securing a new position. But many people shy away from it; after all it doesn't appear to be the most comfortable of activities. Nevertheless, estimates amongst career professionals indicate that between 50 and 70 per cent of people get jobs through their contacts, and this figure rises even higher during a recession. This compares with less than 20 per cent who get their jobs using recruitment agencies or responding to advertising.

It is obvious why networking is even more effective during a recession. The very activity of recruiting someone is expensive so when times are tough and firms are not sure whether they really even need to fill a position, the cost of the recruitment process itself, and the uncertain outcome – not knowing if they will find the right person – can be enough to make them decide against creating a vacancy. However, if you introduce yourself to them, and you have what they need, then there is a possibility that they will decide to give it a go and take you on, albeit on a trial basis.

Networking gets you access to vacancies before they are advertised. Possibly even before they are known. The opportunities iceberg below shows the recruitment process:

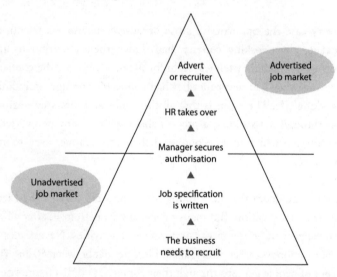

Once the recruitment process is in the hands of the HR department it is becomes much harder to secure an advantage through networking. Try to establish contact while the recruitment process is still in the lower half of the triangle.

Feeling comfortable about networking

It is really important to stress that networking is not about asking strangers to do you favours, or to get you a job. It is far more subtle than that! You are not asking for help, of course that would feel uncomfortable, particularly when it is associated with a job or work. None of us likes to put pressure on people – we don't want to oblige them to do something for us.

So let's be clear. Networking is not about asking and taking. As a networker you have something to offer your contacts, perhaps not now but possibly in the future. Maybe you know someone you can introduce that person to. Networking is a collaborative activity – there is no obligation on you, and you should never feel that there is. If you can help you will, if not, nobody minds. Networking is self-perpetuating. As you do it more, so your network grows and this opens up opportunities that would not otherwise have presented themselves, opportunities that often arise completely out of the blue.

Crucially, people generally like to help others if they can, especially if they can give advice. This is important to bear in mind. When you network you are not asking for a job, you are asking for advice and someone else's expertise. If you ask for a job the process will stall immediately: if someone can't offer you a job they can't help you. If you ask someone a question that leads to a 'no' answer, such as, 'can you help me get a job?', you don't get the chance to ask them again.

The best sort of networking is when you use it to gather information in order to help you make decisions about your career. The conversations you have, and the contacts you make, should lead to potential opportunities. Networking brings you into contact with people in the companies or industries you are targeting. These people will be able to give you advice about, and help you shape, your career ideas and plans. This will make it much easier to evaluate them.

Many of these contacts will know other people who will be able to give you advice. Many of the people you meet will work for potential employers. Through systematic exposure to these people you get closer to possible employment. As your network of contacts widens more and more people will keep you in mind when possible opportunities arise.

Most networking is initiated with existing contacts. This is generally the most effective way to network as you are likely to get more committed help. However, sometimes you don't know anyone with connections to the industries or companies you are exploring. You may therefore need to network speculatively. Rather than initiating the process by contacting somebody you know, you first need to identify potential network contacts who you don't know. You can do this through research.

Networking works because it is collegiate. The person you are talking to knows that when they need to, they can also get in touch with you, to get advice, information or contacts who will be able to help them with their career.

Networking also works because it is empowering and a little bit subversive. Companies may be in competition with each other but you are talking to people, at a human level. It gives both parties an opportunity to break out of the formal constraints of being a company employee, and to talk openly and honestly.

Example script to introduce yourself to a new contact

"Hello. My name is Susan Williams. I was given your name by Jean Vincent who thought you might be able to give me some advice.

"I'm in the process of changing my job and I'm exploring a number of different avenues although I've made no firm decisions yet and have not begun job-hunting seriously. One area I'm looking at is the insurance industry. While I haven't any direct experience of it I feel I have some skills that would transfer into it well and I was hoping to

find out more about how my capabilities could be used in the sector.

"Would you be kind enough to spare 20 minutes or so to allow me to ask you a few questions about this? I'd be happy to meet at a time and place convenient to you."

Think about how you would deal with any resistance or objections that you might meet. If your contact is unwilling to meet you, can they suggest someone else who may be available to help?

Identifying your network

Your network comprises not just business contacts but also friends, family and anyone else you know. A good career consultant will also connect you to their client network. A good way of building your contact list is to draw up category headings and list the people you know in each. The table below will help.

CATEGORY	WHO DO I KNOW?
Friends	
Family	
Neighbours	
Friends I haven't seen for years	
Colleagues	
Former colleagues	
Suppliers/former suppliers	
Customers/former customers	
Sports and social contacts (clubs, community groups, etc.)	
Partner's contacts	
Personal services suppliers (accountant, hairdresser, mechanic, etc).	

You can also look at contacts in terms of type: A contacts are people you know. They refer you to others (B contacts) who have contacts in appropriate places. B contacts are information resources. These people (also known as bridge contacts) are connected to the people who make decisions and may be able to offer a position (C contacts).

The networking steps

Prepare a list of people to network with, using your contacts list as a starting point. It may be that you need to go to directories or other sources if you simply don't know anyone, or enough people, within the area you are exploring. If so, make sure you get the name of a fairly senior person if at all possible.

Initiate contact. Email can be both direct and immediate, provided it is read. Don't expect to always receive a reply though. If you haven't heard back in a week, follow up with a phone call. Telephone risks getting blocked by a gatekeeper (for example a PA, secretary or receptionist). The best way round this is to have an introduction so the person is already expecting the call. Make your call or email brief; outline your situation and what you want – about 20 minutes of their time.

Don't go in too strong. Remember that people like to think they can help or give advice. So all you need to do is suggest a short meeting or conversation because you would like to ask their advice about the industry or company that you feel they can help you with.

Don't send a CV. Even if it might help them to understand the situation, it may cause them to assume you want a job and could make them feel uncomfortable. Or they may simply tell you that the expertise you have picked up in your earlier career is not something they can help you to build on.

Plan! Before you go to the networking meeting, it is essential to plan thoroughly. You might not get a second chance with this contact – and they might turn out to be the most important person you have met in your working life. Don't waste the opportunity!

Identify your objective. What do you want to achieve from the meeting? Information about the industry, information about the work and further contacts are all positive outcomes.

Think about the possible contacts your contact will have. Maybe they have colleagues or clients who work in the sector you are exploring? Prepare for the meeting. Do your research about the organisation. Think in detail about the questions you want to ask. How are you going to present your situation? What messages are you going to project?

At the meeting. Remember, this is your meeting – you initiated it and the agenda is yours so take the lead. Start with a very brief presentation of yourself. Outline your strengths and try to establish how well your contact feels these fit the needs of the industry. Try to find out what other skills are important and what training or formal education you might need. Ask for names of other people who would be worth meeting. You may have particular companies in mind but no names; do they know anyone in those companies you can contact? Leave your own contact details in case they have any other ideas. Do not leave a CV unless they ask for it.

Good networking questions to ask

How did you start in this area?
What are the essential skills required for working in this field?
What other strengths are needed for success?
What are the prospects for the industry?
What organisations are expanding?

What are the main challenges in the job?
What do you most like about the job?
From what do you get your job satisfaction?
What would a typical week involve?
What advice would you offer to someone coming into this business for the first time?
What would you recommend I do to prepare for getting work in this sector?
How do you think my past experience and skills fit into this sector?
What opportunities do you see in the future for this industry?
What companies are you aware of that are looking to recruit?
Who else do you think I ought to talk to in order to find out more about working in this area?

After the meeting

Follow up. You now have a new contact for your network but that person will be lost if you don't nurture the relationship. Email within a couple of days, or even send a card to thank them for giving you the time and acknowledge how useful the meeting was for you. Now may be the time to put your cards on the table and state a commitment to getting into this area of work, if that's the case. Keep in fairly regular contact during the process – perhaps a quick email every fortnight updating people on your progress and inviting them to think if they have any new ideas for you. But make sure you don't overdo it. Nobody likes to hear from someone frequently if they have nothing of real interest to say.

Record the outcome and progress carefully. Note who you saw, their company, when the meeting took place and who introduced you to that person. Outline the key points of the discussion and any contacts they gave you.

Nurture the contact even after you have secured your new position. The real value of networking is keeping the relationship alive even when you are not in need of help. This makes it all the easier to ask for help again in the future. If people only hear from you between jobs what will they think of you? Make yourself available to help people by keeping in touch with them from time to time. For some of your contacts that might mean going for a drink, coffee or a meal every few months, for others, it may mean an occasional update by phone or email.

Presentation statements

We mentioned earlier that when you meet a network contact for the first time you will need to introduce yourself and explain why you have asked for the meeting. This is best done through a presentation statement, or an elevator pitch as it is sometimes called.

This is perhaps the most important part of your job-search toolkit. The name elevator pitch indicates what they are – imagine you get into a lift and discover that the only other person in there is the contact you have been trying for weeks to meet. You have six floors to sell yourself to him. Your elevator pitch is what you will say.

Elevator pitches or presentation statements need to be lively, positive and engaging. They also need to be brief; you don't have much time and you don't want to get caught up with too much detail. What can you say about yourself in thirty seconds that will lead the other person to say, "I'd like to hear more, let's fix up a meeting"?

A good presentation statement should contain the following:
■ An introduction. Who are you, what do you do, why would they be interested in hearing about you? Pretend they have asked you, 'tell me about yourself', but of course they haven't, so be concise and engaging.

■ A little bit about how you got to where you are now, and what you are looking for. It's not your life story, but rather a sentence or two which says something like, 'I have just left my job after five years as Technical Director of XXX and am looking for my next opportunity'.

■ Something about what you are doing to get what you have just said you are looking for. Be positive, describe the energy which you are putting into your job search.

By this time the lift has probably reached the sixth floor and your contact may be walking away. So you quickly need to see if you can fix up a meeting. Obviously this may be too hasty, so if you do get the opportunity to carry on the conversation first, try to do so.

If you can continue the conversation, give an overview of your career to date, your main strengths and abilities and your achievements. Remember you are trying to get them to want to take the conversation forward, so be bullish and positive about yourself – without being arrogant.

Finally, end with a statement that will stick in their mind, which you feel best describes your unique selling point. This is your slogan, it needs some thought but it will be worth it.

3. Online networking

Online or social networking has boomed over the last few years, and there is little sign that its growth is abating. Some social networking sites such as LinkedIn carry job advertisements as part of their service to users. Others, such as Facebook do not have a dedicated job board, but there are plenty of jobs to be found if you use the site in the right way.

The advantages of social networking are that it is quick and easy to extend your network. You don't need to spend time meeting people, your networking is all done online and the question of whether you and the other person like each other or hit it off doesn't really come into it. Once you have set someone up as a contact you generally have indirect access to all their contacts, just as you do if you meet someone and they agree to introduce you to the people they know.

The disadvantage of social networking however is the impersonal element. It is not always easy to form a reliable impression of someone from their online persona. In a quiet job market, when many people find they have time on their hands, social networking sites are likely to experience a significant increase in traffic. Be warned. In a recession the number of bored people sitting in front of their computers increases dramatically. Make sure when you are communicating online that your contacts are worthwhile and not time wasters.

What are the most useful online networking sites?
It's worth spending some time deciding which online networking sites are most appropriate for your job search. This may not be the same site as you use for your leisure time social networking. Each site tends to

concentrate on a different age group and social outlook and you would be well advised to spend time on each to understand which are most likely to present you with contacts that are relevant to your job search and realistic job opportunities.

The most relevant sites for the majority of job seekers are:

LinkedIn
LinkedIn is probably the most career focused of all the social networking sites. It describes itself as an *online network of more than 30 million experienced professionals from around the world, representing 150 industries.*

LinkedIn claims that *through your network you can:*
- *Find potential clients, service providers, subject experts, and partners who come recommended;*
- *Be found for business opportunities;*
- *Search for great jobs;*
- *Discover inside connections who can help you land jobs and close deals;*
- *Get introduced to other professionals through the people you know.*

The site is divided into four sections: People, Jobs, Answers and Companies, indicating a strong emphasis on careers.

Of course it is difficult for you to be visible on any site with millions of members. The key to being seen on LinkedIn is to have as many contacts as you can, and as many recommendations. This means that when you first sign in you need to search the site for people you know and ask them both to connect to you and to give you a recommendation. You will recommend them in return.

Because LinkedIn gives you the ability to search by company, it is easy to find people who work in your target organisations. Once you have found them, you can work out how to contact them. On LinkedIn you contact people through Introductions. Introductions use a mutual connection to introduce two members. You can send an introduction through more than one connection to reach the person you want, although the more contacts your request passes through, the lower the probability that your request will reach its target.

Basic membership of LinkedIn is free but gives you only a limited ability to contact other users. Various levels of premium membership provide greater flexibility in using the service.

Facebook

Probably the best known of all the social networking groups, Facebook provides great opportunities for job search networking. According to the site, *millions of people use Facebook everyday to keep up with friends, upload an unlimited number of photos, share links and videos, and learn more about the people they meet.*

Although Facebook does not offer the facility to search by company, many organisations or their employees have started their own networks, known as groups, on Facebook. For example, if you search for IBM you will come across several groups dedicated to IBM employees, past and present. And, since these are open groups which anyone can join, presumably the membership includes prospective employees as well. Once you join the group you can post messages on the discussion board to find out the company information you need, and you can ask members of the group to become your friend so that you can network directly.

Alternatively you can enter the job you are looking for in the search box and find groups or people who meet your criteria. For example a search for 'graphic designer' produces over 500 groups, 500 people and fifty events all of which are connected in some way to the keyword graphic designer.

Xing

Xing has been operating in Europe for a few years but is only now beginning to make its mark in the UK. The site claims to have over 6.5 million business professionals who use XING to do business and promote their career.

You will need a premium membership to Xing to contact other members, although free membership will allow you to get in touch with those you have nominated as contacts. Unlike LinkedIn, Xing is not currently listing jobs but it does have groups, many of which are based on professional or company membership.

Perhaps the greatest asset that Xing has is its cross-European reach. If you are looking for a role with a European company, you are more likely to find relevant contacts on Xing than on LinkedIn. LinkedIn by contrast has a North American bias.

Online networking – things to beware of

Membership of LinkedIn, Facebook and Xing will provide you with a fully comprehensive online networking strategy. But online networking should be treated with caution. It is very easy to while away hours online, thinking that you are being productive in your networking while in practice all that is happening is that you are whiling away time searching for new contacts without actually getting anywhere.

Then there is the problem of inactive, or false, membership. Every online networking group measures its success in terms of the number of members it has. But in practice many members will have signed up on a whim and never visited the site again. Others may have signed up under a false name, just to see what the site is like, without anyone finding out that they were looking. This means you can waste a lot of time contacting people who will never respond to you. The best way to defend against this is to only get in touch with people whose profile indicates they are active members, with recent updates on their file.

Another thing to watch out for is unscrupulous people who will try to contact you in order to sell you services, or to spam you. When you put your profile online you are making a very public statement about yourself and you do need to exercise some caution in what you say. All the networking sites contain guidelines suggesting how you should present yourself, and sensible precautions to take to protect your privacy. Here are the precautions that LinkedIn recommends:

■ *Only connect to people you know and trust well enough to recommend them to others. This gives you much more control over who can see your profile and who can contact you. It also makes it far more likely that Introduction requests that are forwarded to you will be in line with your interests. Because your direct connections are able to see your most up-to-date primary email address, connecting only to people you trust will help you keep your contact information safe.*

■ *Don't post your email address, phone number, or other addresses on your LinkedIn profile; if you do you'll have much less control over how your contact information can be used.*

■ *Familiarise yourself with your current personal privacy and contact settings on LinkedIn so you know what they are and what options you have. To view these settings visit your Account & Settings found at the top of your homepage.*

- *Select a password for LinkedIn that can't easily be guessed. Create one that includes 10 or more characters and includes both letters and numbers.*

- *Never give your LinkedIn password to others.*

- *If you use a public or shared computer to log into LinkedIn make sure you log out completely when you've finished.*

- *Report privacy problems that you see or experience on LinkedIn to Customer Service.*

Making online networking part of your recession job search strategy

None of the above should put you off using online networking, it is an important part of your online toolkit. But do make sure that you integrate it well with your personal networking and other strategies. Nothing is more valuable than face to face networking with trusted contacts, online relationships rarely generate the same quality of contact.

Try to restrict the amount of time you spend online. It can be addictive and a real time waster. Check your inboxes no more than once or twice a day, unless you are waiting for a particularly urgent message. If people do not respond to you, don't waste time chasing them; try a different route to get the information you need. It is a tough job market out there. You have a lot to do. Use your time wisely.

Don't be put off by doom and gloom reports in the press about the deepening recession. It is bound to happen; but there are plenty of jobs out there. If you don't believe me just take a look around LinkedIn and Xing. You will come across dozens of people who are reporting that they have a new job. By keeping your head above water you can become one of them.

Building your opportunity list

Once you have started to develop your network you should begin to hear about job opportunities through your grapevine. You will also start to hear of opportunities as a result of the reactive methods you are using, which we discussed earlier.

It is a good idea to keep track of these opportunities. If they start coming in thick and fast you will want to be sure that you have a good overview of what you need to do about each one, and when. If there are not as many opportunities as you had hoped, a good record of where each one came from, and when, will help you to plan what to do in order to generate more.

Draw up a chart like this, or use a computer spreadsheet:

OPPORTUNITY			STATUS				
Company	Role	Source? (e.g. network contact, recruiter, advert, etc.)	Date of Application	Application acknow-ledged?	First interview date?	Second interview date?	Next action?

If your opportunity list looks thin you can add to it by making speculative applications to companies for which you know you have something to offer, even though you do not know if they have any vacancies. We will cover this in chapters 8 and 9.

Applying for a job

4. Understanding what you offer

A marketing approach

Getting a job is a marketing exercise; it is no different from any other. Think of it in exactly the same way as you would think about bringing a new product or service onto the market. You need to know what the new service offers, and where the market is for it. The only difference is that the service is you and the market is those organisations who could potentially be interested in obtaining your services.

A recession requires companies to be that much smarter in understanding their market, and the value that their product offers; you too will need to be that bit smarter in understanding what it is that you offer, and who out there is likely to want it. Whether you are bringing a new product to market, or marketing yourself, the key preparatory steps you need to follow are:

■ Define what you offer;
■ Identify the market that needs and wants your services;
■ Understand what needs are not being met in that market that you can additionally fill and
■ Determine the benefits you offer.

Defining what you offer

Your offer to the employer consists of three main elements:
■ Your skills;
■ Your experience;
■ Your qualifications.

What are my skills?

There is a lot of talk in job hunting circles about transferable skills. These are capabilities that you can use as easily in one job as in another. The art of verbal communication is a transferable skill, it can be used in many jobs. Carpentry is a skill that is not really transferable; there are a few jobs where it comes in handy but its only real value is if you are a carpenter.

To begin with let's take the emphasis off transferable skills. We will just talk about skills. Because all skills are worth taking into account when applying for a job, even if, as in the case of carpentry, they seem to pigeonhole you. In fact carpentry is not a limited skill at all! A good carpenter uses a number of skills. These include manual dexterity, spatial intelligence, accuracy, planning and both geometric and arithmetic calculation.

A carpenter may also have organisational, administrative or managerial skills, particularly if he has been self-employed. His skill set may include driving, or negotiating with customers and suppliers.

So rather than thinking that what you offer is a complex skill like carpentry, think of your skills in small chunks. There may be few carpentry jobs when the construction sector is hard in a recession but there will be many more jobs that require at least some of the skills that make up carpentry.

Here are some exercises that will help you identify some of your skills. The first one is based on what you consider to be your greatest personal achievements, because when you are achieving you are using your top skills at their very best. Let's take a closer look at this.

Skills exercise 1: my achievements

For this exercise you need to spend some time thinking about the times when you felt a real sense of achievement. This might include anything you found particularly satisfying and felt proud of, or a challenge you successfully overcame.

Use pages 43 to 48 to outline six things that you regard as particular achievements in your life so far. You don't need to restrict these to workplace achievements but try to ensure that at least two of your achievements are work related. Before you start, read through the box on pages 41-42 which should help you to identify your achievements. Here's an example.

The situation

As project administrator I was responsible for managing the budget for a two year project involving 40 people. During a particularly hot spell I noticed that the cost of bottled water was quite high as we were buying it in from a local shop and half full bottles were being thrown away.

The action taken

I looked into finding a supplier which would make buying in water cheaper and less time-consuming. A deal was set up whereby a company would supply cold water units and regularly deliver full, and collect empty, canisters.

The outcome or result

The annual cost of water was reduced by 40% with zero wastage. Water consumption increased slightly with a slight decrease in consumption of hot beverages, resulting in a time and cost saving. Increased satisfaction among the workforce and time saved in not having to go to the shop to buy water.

The skills and qualities I used.

Initiative, communication and persuasion, analysis of costs, research, negotiation.

The way I felt afterwards

Capable and effective, but not recognised.

Identifying your achievements

We tend to overlook our achievements – those things we have done in our professional and personal lives that really made us feel good about ourselves. It may be because we are modest or we have never taken the time to reflect upon our successes. Achievements can be at work, in your personal life or as a result of your hobbies. An achievement is at least one of the following:

■ Something you have done for which you have been recognised or rewarded;
■ Something which you are proud of having accomplished;
■ Something you have done which has surpassed expectation;
■ Something that has benefited yourself or others.

Think about your work experience and your life in general, identify up to six experiences that you initiated or participated in significantly. Include experiences in which you performed well and found satisfying. Do your best to identify at least four work experiences, and also include some from your personal life.

Give each experience a shorthand name so you can easily recall it for yourself. Think of each experience in terms of:

■ The challenge or problem situation;
■ The action you took;
■ The result.

Write a description or story of the experience in specific detail.
- What did you do?
- What were the obstacles you overcame?
- How did you know you were successful?

The following are some questions to help you think more specifically about your achievements and their results. What have you done that has:
- Led to a new skill?
- Increased your knowledge?
- Given you personal satisfaction?
- Completed a significant task?
- Added value to your organisation?
- Benefited someone in your team?
- Achieved an objective?
- Resulted in specific rewards e.g. money, promotion or more responsibility?
- Increased your reputation in the company or your community?

Has something been:
- Improved, Increased, Reduced, Streamlined, Simplified, Broadened, Changed?

Have you been able to do something:
- Faster, Slower, Cheaper, More Accurately, Bigger, Smaller?

Have you done something to lead to better:
- Sales, Quality, Cost, Timeframes, Productivity?

What were the results of the Achievement for the organisation? What impact did the achievement have on sales, morale, turnover, productivity, communications, culture, training, public relations, image, profitability, market, and products/services?

Achievement 1

The situation

The action taken

The outcome or result

The skills and qualities I used

The way I felt afterwards

Achievement 2

The situation

The action taken

The outcome or result

The skills and qualities I used

The way I felt afterwards

Achievement 3

The situation

The action taken

The outcome or result

The skills and qualities I used

The way I felt afterwards

Achievement 4

The situation

The action taken

The outcome or result

The skills and qualities I used

The way I felt afterwards

Achievement 5

The situation

The action taken

The outcome or result

The skills and qualities I used

The way I felt afterwards

Achievement 6

The situation

The action taken

The outcome or result

The skills and qualities I used

The way I felt afterwards

Skills exercise 2: my skills audit

We all have natural skills and abilities and learn new skills through paid employment, voluntary work and through leisure and social activities. It is common to undervalue our skills and we can forget that our skills are transferable. The following exercise will help you to focus more specifically on the types of tasks and activities that you enjoy and will most likely perform well at work. In addition, when you are clear about your skills, you will be able to communicate them more effectively to a potential employer.

1. *Using the competency rating scale of 1–4, rate yourself against the skills listed in the table overleaf. Please try to overcome any modesty and be as objective as you can. Think also about feedback you have had from others, such as managers at work, teachers, family or friends.*

2. *Use the second and third columns to tick those skills you particularly enjoy using (maximum of 25) and those you would like to develop in the future.*

3. *Please leave the fourth column blank for now.*

Skill competency rating scale:
1 = *Undeveloped*
2 = *Adequate*
3 = *Competent*
4 = *Very competent*

Skill type	Skill competency (rate 1–4)	Skills I enjoy using (tick)	Skills I'd like to develop (tick)	Skills used in achievements (tick)
People skills				
Interviewing others for information				
Facilitating group discussions, meetings				
Building teams				
Representing others				
Advising others				
Leading others				
Mediating, resolving conflict				
Managing, supervising others				
Coaching, motivating others				
Actively listening, assessing needs				
Caring for others				
Empathising, conveying warmth to others				
Serving others				
Training, teaching others				
Presenting, performing in front of a group				
Speaking in a foreign language				
Entertaining, amusing others				
Meeting new people				
Putting others at ease				
Building and maintaining relationships				
Influencing, persuading others				
Negotiating with others				
Selling goods or ideas to others				

Skill type	Skill competency (rate 1–4)	Skills I enjoy using (tick)	Skills I'd like to develop (tick)	Skills used in achievements (tick)
Information skills				
Researching, gathering information				
Investigating, finding out the facts				
Observing, examining people, trendwatching				
Analysing information, data				
Classifying and recording information				
Interpreting and explaining				
Reviewing and evaluating				
Writing clearly and concisely				
Editing, summarising information				
Planning tasks, projects				
Managing knowledge, information				
Administering tasks				
Organising resources, information				
Managing projects, events				
Paying attention to detail				
Problem solving, troubleshooting				
Improving systems and procedures				
Assessing risks, probabilities				
Making decisions under pressure				
Operating computers, using IT				
Working with numbers, statistics				
Budgeting, costing, managing money				
Forecasting, predicting				
Seeing ways to save time or money				

Skill type	Skill competency (rate 1–4)	Skills I enjoy using (tick)	Skills I'd like to develop (tick)	Skills used in achievements (tick)
Practical/physical skills				
Constructing, building, assembling				
Installing, fitting, adapting				
Making, crafting things, materials				
Fixing, repairing machines, equipment				
Operating, controlling, maintaining				
Handling tools				
Driving vehicles				
Manual dexterity				
Hand-eye coordination				
Playing a musical instrument				
Physical fitness, strength				
Other skills				

Skill type	Skill competency (rate 1–4)	Skills I enjoy using (tick)	Skills I'd like to develop (tick)	Skills used in achievements (tick)
Information skills				
Innovating, creating new solutions				
Imagining new ideas, concepts, alternatives				
Thinking laterally				
Developing the ideas of others				
Creating new systems and procedures				
Designing a plan for a project or object				
Designing using shapes, spaces, colours				
Designing machines, technology				
Writing creatively				
Drawing, painting				
Composing music				
Using intuition, insight				
Initiating, starting up new projects				
Improvising under pressure				
Assessing situations and people quickly and accurately				
Thinking strategically, seeing the bigger picture				
Observing, interpreting patterns and trends				

Highlight in some way on your table those skills in which you have rated yourself as 'Competent' or 'Very competent' in the first column and that you have indicated in the second column that you enjoy using. Note which skill types these generally fall into. You might want to discuss the results with a friend who knows you well.

If your list is very long, create a shorter list below of the top 10 skills that you enjoy using the most and for which you have given yourself a competency rating of 3 or 4.

Specific skill	Skill type (people, information, ideas or practical)
1.	
2.	
3.	
4.	
5.	
6.	
7.	
8.	
9.	
10.	

Skills exercise 3: linking your skills and achievements

Now go back to the achievements exercise and review each one in turn. Note down the key skills you used for each achievement, up to a maximum of 5 each. For example, if your achievement was to resolve a long running dispute between two colleagues, you may have used persuading, empathising and problem solving skills.

Achievement	Key skills used
1.	
2.	
3.	
4	
5.	
6.	

Now add up the number of times each skill occurs. List the ten skills that occur most frequently below.

By linking your skills and achievements in this way you can give examples to potential employers of the skills you possess. Employers want to know your key skills and need you to provide them with actual evidence that you have those skills. That is, specific examples when you have successfully used your skills to produce a beneficial outcome for yourself, for others or your organisation.

Finally, go back to the answers you wrote in the 'achievements' section of the initial assessment on page 43-48. Look at the skills that you said you have used. Bearing in mind what we said above about carpentry, can you break any of these skills down into smaller units? Look again at the actual achievement. Are there other, more specialised skills that you can include now that you see how large skills can be made up of smaller ones? Write all these skills in a column on the left hand side of a separate sheet of paper. Head the column 'My top skills'.

Now let's consider your everyday skills. You may not have used these skills when you were carrying out one of your achievements, but they are just as important. There are many ways to identify your everyday skills. The easiest way is to make a list of all the tasks you regularly perform – you may find it easier to keep a diary for a few days. Consider which skills you are using when performing these tasks. Write them down in the same column as your top skills, under the heading 'Everyday skills'.

Finally we need to consider your undeveloped skills. These are not so easy to spot. They may be skills that you used as a child, or even skills you have never used, but just suspect that you have. Think back to episodes from your childhood, or memorable events as an adult. Can you see yourself acting in a particularly capable or talented way in any of these episodes? If so, what skill might you have been using? Write it down in the same column, under the heading 'Undeveloped skills'.

Now draw up a second column on the same sheet. Head it 'Want to use'. And a third column 'Don't want to use.

Your sheet of paper should look something like this:

My top skills	Want to use	Don't want to use
My everyday skills		
My undeveloped skills		

You know what to do next! Mark those skills that you would like to use in your future career. And those that you don't want to use. Be brave. If you have to change your job because of the recession, you might as well aim for a job that lets you do the things you enjoy doing, and doesn't force you to do the things you hate. If you are a saleswoman and you don't want to use the skill of persuasion any more, say so. You can always add an unwanted skill back into your list of skills you have to use, if necessary. You probably won't need to though.

You may well want help with naming your skills, or you may want to complete some exercises to help you identify even more skills that you may have. There are loads of resources on the internet, in libraries and elsewhere. You will find skills lists on the internet as well as questionnaires to help you identify what you are good at. Some will be better than others. Don't pay for anything though, there is enough good free stuff around.

5. Responding to job advertisements

I met a man recently who seemed to have exactly the right approach to the recession. He was out of work and was supremely confident that he would not get another job any time soon. But this did not seem to bother him a bit. Even though he enjoyed his work, and was quite frank about the fact that had he not lost his job he would not have come to see me, he had no regrets about being unemployed right now. "I see this as an opportunity", he said. "There are many things I have not yet done, that I would like to do, and I need your help in exploring these and deciding which direction to go in. Much as I would have been happy to carry on with what I was doing, this recession has given me the chance to take a step back, re-evaluate, and add a new dimension to my life." He had decided that he did not want to look for a job right now. Instead, he wanted to spend the next few months planning a new career for himself.

Unfortunately, this approach will not suit most people. Much as you might like to sit out the recession, there is almost certainly an economic imperative for you to return to work as quickly as possible. And although we have already said that networking is the most likely route to a new job, in order to network well it helps to have written a few job applications and to be clear in your mind exactly what your messages are.

So we will start by looking at how to apply for the jobs that you will come across in press adverts and on internet job boards. Advertised jobs frequently get hundreds of people responding to them depending on the speciality and seniority of the position. In the current climate some jobs will get thousands of applications. So of course it is bound to be a bit of a lottery – not even the most conscientious recruiter can screen and prioritise that many applications accurately.

Usually anything up to 80% of the responses fail to match the criteria in the advertisement. You need to make sure that your response stands out from the crowd so that you get screened in rather than screened out. This means that both your covering letter and your CV need to be modified to address the specific requirements of the advert and to ensure that there is nothing in your response that could be a turn-off for the person screening the applications. Realistically, just to survive the first screening, you must meet most of the qualifications mentioned and be able to demonstrate how well you meet them. This is in spite of the fact that in many adverts the required competencies are a bit of a wish list and the employer is unlikely to find someone who meets them all. General rules for answering adverts are:

■ Respond from 3–4 days after the advert appears, rather than immediately. You will have a better chance of being noticed;

■ Be brief and focus on the advertiser's expressed needs;

■ Address each letter to a person wherever possible;

■ Always write a letter that outlines both the explicit and implicit requirements from the advertisement. Show how you meet or exceed these needs. You may wish to use a two-column approach for this section of your letter. On the left list the requirements in the advert and on the right the skills and abilities you possess that meet these needs. If you can demonstrate that you meet 60–70 per cent of the criteria (bearing in mind the wish list principle we mentioned above) then you should apply.

If at all possible do not send your salary history, even if it is requested. Instead state that your salary expectations are flexible and that your current package is consistent with the market. If you know or can identify the person in the company responsible for the position, write to them in addition to responding to the person or department mentioned in the advert. Indicate that you have already responded to the advert as instructed, and are taking this opportunity to introduce yourself in a more personal way. Follow this up with a phone call about a week after mailing your letter and CV.

Analysing a job advertisement

A typical advertisement will contain:

A statement about the organisation even in a blind advert where the identity is protected:

'Our client is an award-winning, market-leading food manufacturer. Following the recent appointment of a new Chief Executive, it is undertaking a major change initiative to build further market share.'

A statement about the job:

'Reporting to the marketing manager and managing a team of professionals you will be responsible for all marketing functions. This requires the ability to lead from the front and implement the required changes for the new computer system. This role has responsibility for advertising and promotion as well as departmental accountability for budget and employees.'

A list of selection criteria:

'A graduate with professional qualifications from the relevant institute, you will require strong people skills, a capacity to lead remote teams and manage multiple projects. The best candidates will have proven communication and negotiation skills.'

Details:

These include contact details and how to apply. There is usually an idea of the company's location and often some indication of salary and benefits (if the company is named in the advert you can find out more from their web site).

Before you apply

Before you respond to an advertisement prepare some specific questions that are not answered in the advert and phone the company or the agency. If the information is not in the advert, ask for the name, title and correct spelling of the contact person. However, when you phone make sure you are not interviewed on the telephone. If it seems that is happening, make an excuse, agree another time to ring and go away and prepare.

Writing an application letter

Some of the following might seem obvious but it is worth checking through this list. You know how easy it is to make mistakes.

■ Be sure to include your own contact details. Many of us are used to writing on letterhead and forget that we need to include our own address.

■ Make sure you have the recipient's name and address right. Address them by title unless you have spoken to them, when you may feel (but not necessarily) that you can use their first name. Avoid Dear Sir/Madam unless you have no information on the person.

■ Give the complete job reference/number from the ad. If you have had a phone discussion refer to that.

■ Make sure you have done your research. At very least you should have looked at the company's web site. Better still is to have used a corporate research site to do some in-depth research on the company. The more you know about them, what is going on in the company at present, what their needs and goals are, the more targeted a letter you can write.

■ Outline briefly your ability to meet the needs of the job. One effective way is to use a table or bullet points to show a correlation between your experience and the selection criteria shown.

■ Include a paragraph explaining why you are interested in the position, but focus on the advantage to them of employing you, not the advantage to you. Avoid phrases like 'I feel that I am right for this job' or 'I would very much like to have this job'. Talk about what they need and why you fill it.

■ Use a positive close, particularly if you are applying for a sales position. For example 'I will call you in a few days to discuss my application'. This is much more forceful than 'I look forward to hearing from you'.

■ Most business letters and letters of application close with 'Yours sincerely'. Only use 'Yours faithfully' if you do not know the recipients name and have addressed the letter to 'Dear Sir/Madam'.

■ The letter should be a maximum of one page long. Remember the recipients spend a minimum time reading your responses.

■ Revise your CV to highlight all the achievements relevant to this application and include it with your letter.

■ Always write a new letter for each application. Even if you have a template that you base your letter on, make sure you consider each letter separately. That way your letters will be fresh and alive, not dull and mass produced.

■ Remember that your letter and your CV are the only things they know about you. They have to be good!

Sample advertisement response letters

20 Hill View Crescent
Winchester
Hants
SO62 2HU

Mr Donald Jones
Human Resources Director
Wavelength Industries
100 North Road
Southampton
Hants SO53 2XS
25 May 2009

Dear Mr Jones

I wish to apply for the role of Accounting Supervisor as advertised in The Times on 20 May 2009.

I believe that I have the skills and experience to assist Wavelength Industries (refer here to whatever you feel is relevant in the company's activities or current news stories). I outline below my experience as it matches your requirements.

Your needs	My experience and skills
Three to five years of accounting experience	Five years in-depth accounting experience in progressively senior roles. ACCA qualified in 2002. Reduced costs in departments supported by 5% year on year. Managed staff of three professionals.
Strong analytical skills	Proven excellence in analysing complex business accounts with a view to making informed recommendations. Undertook detailed audit inventory of processes leading to better streamlined processes and significant savings of £50,000.
Knowledge of accounting systems	Experienced in day-to-day, month and year end processing. Super user for SAP implementation involved in defining user requirements. Developed and implemented a new purchase order system using new software resulting in increased cost control and greater reporting accuracy.

I have additional relevant accomplishments explained in depth in my attached CV.

I will contact you within the next few days to further discuss my application and arrange an opportunity to meet.

Yours sincerely

Signature

(Name)

20 Hill View Crescent
Winchester
Hants
SO62 2HU
25 May 2009

Mr Donald Jones
Human Resources Director
Wavelength Industries
100 North Road
Southampton
Hants SO53 2XS

Dear Mr Jones

I wish to apply for the role of Accounting Supervisor as advertised in *The Times* on 20 May 2009. I outline below my experience as it matches your requirements.

I am ACCA qualified and have five years in-depth accounting experience in progressively senior roles. In my most recent role as Finance Manager for Dolby Investments Ltd, I manage a team of three professionals and reduced costs across departments by 5% year on year.

My strong analytical skills have enabled me to excel at analysing complex business accounts with a view to making informed recommendations. For example, at Dolby I undertook a detailed audit inventory of processes which lead to a more streamlined system and significant savings of £50,000.

I am experienced in day-to-day, month and year-end processing and a super user for SAP implementation involved in defining user requirements. I have also developed and implemented a new purchase order system using new software resulting in increased cost control and greater reporting accuracy.

I have additional relevant accomplishments explained in my attached CV.
I look forward to hearing from you shortly about my application.
Yours sincerely

Signature

(Name)

6. Writing an effective CV

The importance of keeping your CV up-to-date

If you are like most people you will almost certainly have paid no attention to your CV since the last time you applied for a job. And, like most people,when you do update your CV you will probably be tempted just to add an extra paragraph at the top, detailing the job you have just left, and to not touch the rest of the CV at all.

That is how things used to be done. But if that is all you do, it will put you at a great disadvantage today. A modern CV is a work in progress. It needs to be kept up-to-date; not just by adding your most recent job, but by continually refining the image of yourself that you want your CV to project. Firstly, by adding material when it is fresh in your mind, you will almost certainly be able to present it in a better way. Secondly, remember that opportunity can come along at any moment. The first thing that anyone who floats an opportunity past you will ask for is a copy of your CV. As you will see as we delve more deeply into the whole topic of CVs, you don't want to have to send them a half baked, hastily written draft. And finally because, recession or not, redundancy is a fact of life these days. Even when times are good, let alone in the current climate, you can suddenly find yourself out of a job.

Your CV is a marketing document

Your CV is likely to be the first piece of information that an employer or recruiter will see about you. Since they are likely to receive dozens, if not hundreds of CVs every day, particularly during a recession, your CV needs to stand out. It has to be good.

The ability to express your experience on paper is essential for every job search campaign. A curriculum vitae is not just a historical account of your work history. It is a selling document. What you write on paper may be a deciding factor in gaining you an interview, but it will never get you a job. You will do that yourself through developing contacts and effectively presenting yourself in interviews.

What your CV does however do is:
- Identifies and summarises your abilities and experience and relates them to the actual needs of the job for which you are applying.

- Presents your major accomplishments and achievements in a way that is relevant to your next career move.

- Provides concrete information about you, especially what you consider important about yourself and what you would like others to know.

- Provides a positive 'reminder' of you.

The purpose of the CV is to stimulate interest in you; it is a door opener. It is written to meet the needs of the reader and not to meet your needs and is designed to create a response from the reader such as, 'We need to talk with this person'.

A CV must be truthful. A recent survey revealed that 64% of applicants are willing to invent information for their job search, but most employers are careful to check backgrounds these days. Therefore any statement that could be construed as an embellishment or an untruth will cost you.

There are different styles of CV. It is important to choose a style that is relevant to your career history and the job you are applying for. There is no one way to write your CV and you should ensure that yours reflects not only your background but also your individuality. You can choose different formats for your CV depending on your career objective. Here is an overview of the main formats.

Responsibilities CVs are usually written in job description style, emphasising title and responsibilities. These CVs indicate nothing about achievement, competence and worth. In other words, they tell the reader what you were supposed to do, not what you actually achieved. It is far better to communicate your skills and your achievements to catch the eye of the reader and suggest that their investment in you will be worthwhile.

Chronological CVs start with a summary of your experience and your key skills. This is followed by your work history, beginning with, and placing most emphasis on, your most recent jobs. All achievements are placed beneath the jobs during which they were completed.

Functional CVs start with your achievements, followed by your work experience. The achievements need to be relevant to the job for which you are applying. This gives a clear indication of how your total experience across the years relates to the role. It is especially useful in a recession, when you may be applying into a completely different field of work and your work history may not immediately highlight what you have to offer.

Skills CVs are useful when you are applying for jobs which require knowledge of specific technologies, crafts or software packages. They contain lists of all the technologies that you have worked on or are qualified in.

Industry specific CVs Some industries, for example media or law, use very specific formats that describe the programmes or cases that you have worked on.

You will find examples of the main CV formats on pages 84–89.

Making your CV readable

These are the key points to keep in mind as you write your CV:

■ Keep it short. It should be two pages at most in length. People are busy, they don't have time to read things. There is nothing that you need to communicate in a CV which would necessitate it going beyond two pages. The most successful people tend to have one page CVs; it is quite clear from the small amount of information they need to communicate what they are capable of.

■ It should be easy on the eye. This means making it visually pleasing with quite a bit of white space to make it easy to read.

■ Avoid unusual fonts, tables, photos and graphics. Most CVs are circulated electronically these days, and not everyone has the same defaults on their word processing package. Your CV might look completely different on somebody else's computer. There is nothing worse when trying to read a CV than to be presented with a document in which the information is higgledy piggledy because of over use of fancy word processing techniques.

■ Sentences should be concise and to the point. Use action words and active rather than passive verbs – i.e. things you actually did rather than were done around you. Avoid using pronouns (I, we...) by using bullet points and not full sentences. Don't write about yourself in the third person.

■ Try to be clear about your contributions especially when you are describing what you did as a team member. Verbs such as assisted and co-ordinated can dilute the impact of your efforts.

The structure of your CV

You will find a worksheet to help you with your CV at the end of this chapter. But have a read through the following pages first.

1. Heading

The heading is your contact information presented at the top of the CV. It is not necessary to put the title 'Curriculum Vitae' or 'CV' at the top of the page. In the heading include:

■ Name
■ Home Address
■ Telephone number
■ Email

2. Profile

This is probably the most important part of your CV. It is the first thing that the reader will look at, and if it doesn't grab their attention they won't read on. So make it good. It needs to explain the key skills you have that are relevant to the role for which you are applying. It should be a maximum of three sentences. It supports the credibility of your application and gives the reader an idea of who you are before they read halfway down the page. The profile normally includes some or all of the following:

■ Your experience in the field into which you are selling yourself;
■ Areas of business or industry in which you have worked;
■ Outstanding aspects of your work;
■ Strengths;
■ Relevant skills.

The profile answers the question, *'What are two or three most important facts I want the reader to know about me?'*

Whatever you say in the profile should be supported by evidence in the career history that you will write below. Avoid generalisations and adjectives like 'committed', 'enthusiastic' and 'dynamic'. They are easy to say but difficult to prove. You can also include as part of the profile a career objective – a sentence showing the type of role you are looking for – but generally it is better to leave this for the covering letter. Here are a few examples:

Over seven years' experience in marketing administration in the oil industry. Proven skills in planning, analysis and reporting.

A professional media executive with consultancy experience, differentiated by knowledge of best-practice, operations awareness and excellent people and change management skills.

An experienced executive secretary with strong planning and administrative competence. Proven organisational ability supported by good communication skills. Able to work independently, work to deadlines and to make well judged decisions.

A versatile and committed team leader from the hotel and hospitality industry. Communicates well and is able quickly to establish working relationships at all levels.

3. Key skills or achievements

Depending on the CV format that you have chosen, the next section will list out either your top skills or your top achievements. These should be in bullet points with brief evidence of the work you have done that support your assertions. These bullet points should ideally be tailored to the job applied for so that you can maximise the impact of the first half page of your CV.

4. Career history

This is an account of your experience that includes the names of companies, your job titles, dates of employment and the specific achievements that you attained in each job.

- List your work history in reverse order, starting with current job and giving the name of the company, department, your job title and the dates of employment.

- If your title is specialist to that company or department, use a functional title or explanation in brackets.

- Emphasise the company names by underlining them, capitalising them, or printing them in bold characters.

- Put your employment dates, showing month and year.

- Concentrate on the most recent jobs and summarise earlier jobs.

- Add one or two sentences that summarise the role in terms of its scope: area covered, number of staff, budget responsibility, etc. Be concise.

Focus on achievements

The most important information for each role is a list of your achievements.

By emphasising your achievements rather than your responsibilities, you are demonstrating that you made a difference for the organisation, and that you had a positive impact. You are selling yourself short if you merely state your responsibilities. Anyone can be responsible for something – it does not mean they are any good at it.

The reader wants to know what you actually did during your time in the role. You risk being perceived as an average employee and average employees may have fewer opportunities. An impressive listing of achievements can distinguish you. Achievements are the single most effective element in creating value. Here are some examples of achievement statements:

- Developed and implemented filing system for fifty-person department, resulting in 25 per cent reduction in retrieval time.

- Streamlined office supply purchasing, resulting in a more efficient operation and a saving of £25,000 per year.

- Represented department on customer service task force for six months.

- Set up system that expedited customer complaint handling by 2 per cent.

- Developed and implemented an induction program for all new employees entering our department.

- Recommended a new procedure that reduced the backlog for loan applications by 15 per cent.

- Developed and implemented productivity standards with a PC-based monitoring system, resulting in an efficiency saving of £180,000.

- Reduced uncollected aged accounts, resulting in increased revenue.

■ Designed restructuring plan, resulting in the consolidation of two customer service areas, reducing expenses by £60,000.

■ Managed portfolio of three hundred customers increasing sales by 30 per cent.

■ Organised and trained a sales force for selected marketing territories which increased sales and profits by 60 per cent.

■ Initiated a membership update system for a major non-profit organisation that reduced return mail by 30 per cent.

■ Created an employee training film library to upgrade the skills of fifty staff members. Results revealed that 100 per cent of staff used services, so this increased their training skills by 65 per cent.

■ Increased customer value by working with teams to continually improve order entry and delivery systems.

■ Through establishment of guidelines and procedures, stabilised monthly flow of data input at near-perfect levels for over 18 months.

■ Enhanced customer relationships by instituting targeted selection system for selecting new employees in customer contact positions.

■ Planned and implemented an office filing system; reducing the time required for locating information by 50 per cent.

■ Set up a bookkeeping system reducing the amount of time to prepare payroll by 50 hours.

- Retained 50 per cent of customers through an innovative tracking system to assist sales representatives in customer follow-up.

- Led a team effort that cut substantial costs, enhanced customer value and retained valuable employees in key strategic positions.

- Planned, developed and managed execution of all direct mail and telemarketing programs for Credit Insurance Business; increased penetration of credit card base by 10 per cent in 2002; exceeded plan revenues by £700M.

- Within highly competitive market conditions, planned, developed and managed execution of all print and direct mail programs for National Deposit Business; increased portfolio by 25 per cent and achieved average deposits of over £40 million.

- Developed and implemented strategies for free insurance services (merchandise protection, common carrier, car rental coverage, etc.); achieved savings of £600 million the following year; obtained approval for additional savings of £160 million through an exit strategy.

- Managed a small business team for retail customers that achieved one thousand sales calls within a short time period. Efforts resulted in £1 million additional deposits in chequing accounts, certificates of deposit and mutual funds.

- Worked with marketing support areas to develop brochures and marketing materials by demonstrating initiative to complete the project on time and within budget. Brochure resulted in one hundred additional cash management applications.

■ As a team member, designed and implemented a sales programme that resulted in five hundred calls and four hundred referrals to produce larger market share and maintain existing customers.

Writing your achievement statements

A good achievement statement contains the following parts:

■ An action verb describing what you did rather than your responsibilities.

■ The results of your activities, given in measurements, such as numbers, per cent, amounts of money, or value-added results for customers. Show how the organisation and other team members benefited. This will avoid a 'So what?' attitude on the part of the listener.

■ The scope of your activities (e.g. size of unit, size of budget managed or number of personnel affected).

All achievement statements will serve as examples or proof of your skills. They will show why you are the right fit for the job you are applying for. In a good CV you would expect to have ten to fifteen achievement statements. Wherever you include achievements, put the strongest and most important ones first. Try not to include achievements more than about ten years old unless they are relevant in supporting your qualifications for the job you are applying for.

You should find the following guidelines useful for writing your achievement statements:

■ Keep them to no more than two typewritten lines. Remember, people don't read long paragraphs.

■ Keep it simple. Translate technical jargon so someone without your expertise can understand it.

■ Avoid specialist abbreviations wherever you can.

■ Do not include confidential information about any former employers.

■ Do not lie or exaggerate any of your achievements.

The action words in the box on page 77 can help you write your achievement statements.

Action word list

Accomplished	Developed	Investigated	Selected
Achieved	Devised	Issued	Serviced
Acted	Directed	Launched	Set up
Administered	Discussed	Led	Signed
Adopted	Disseminated	Made	Simplified
Advised	Doubled	Maintained	Sold
Analysed	Drafted	Managed	Solved
Anticipated	Earned	Negotiated	Sparked
Appraised	Edited	Notified	Staffed
Approved	Eliminated	Observed	Started
Arranged	Enabled	Obtained	Stimulated
Ascertained	Established	Operated	Streamlined
Assembled	Evaluated	Organised	Strengthened
Assisted	Examined	Originated	Stressed
Assumed	Executed	Participated	Stretched
Assured	Exercised	Performed	Structured
Attended	Expanded	Planned	Studied
Audited	Expedited	Prepared	Submitted
Authorised	Facilitated	Processed	Succeeded
Balanced	Followed up	Produced	Superseded
Built	Formulated	Promoted	Supervised
Calculated	Fostered	Proposed	Surveyed
Checked	Founded	Provided	Terminated
Circulated	Furnished	Purchased	Traced
Collaborated	Generated	Received	Tracked
Collected	Guided	Recommended	Traded
Compiled	Headed	Recorded	Trained
Completed	Implemented	Redesigned	Transferred
Conducted	Improved	Reduced	Transformed
Consolidated	Improvised	Released	Translated
Consulted	Increased	Reorganised	Trimmed
Controlled	Informed	Reported	Tripled
Converted	Initiated	Represented	Uncovered
Co-operated	Innovated	Required	Unified
Coordinated	Inspected	Researched	Unravelled
Correlated	Installed	Resolved	Utilised
Created	Instituted	Reviewed	Vacated
Cut	Instructed	Revised	Verified
Delegated	Interpreted	Saw	Widened
Delivered	Interviewed	Scanned	Withdrew
Demonstrated	Introduced	Scheduled	Won
Determined	Inventoried	Secured	Worked

5. Education

In most cases this section should be brief, with one line of type for each academic or vocational qualification you have received. Include relevant training courses that you have been on. However, if you are applying for an academic post, or if you are a school leaver or graduate without any significant work history, then this section should be promoted above the career history section.

■ List your highest qualification first.

■ Give the date, the name of the institution or school you studied at, the subjects you studied and the qualifications you obtained.

■ Include formal education qualifications and training programs that are directly related to the job you are applying for.

■ Be concise and relevant. For example, if you are 50 years old with a PhD, don't bother to list your A level or O level grades.

■ If you are currently studying, list the study details and then write in progress.

6. Your interests and hobbies

This is possibly the most overlooked of all sections on most CVs. Yet it tells the reader so much about you. You probably won't have a lot of space left by this stage but it is well worth setting out your hobbies and interests in such a way as to make the reader feel you are an interesting person and well worth meeting. Include your voluntary activities, sporting achievements, sponsored events and charitable fund raising.

7. Additional data (optional)

If you have any relevant technical or specialised skills this is the place to list them. But don't list irrelevant skills just for the sake of it; it takes up valuable CV space and tells the reader nothing.

Memberships or affiliations that are relevant to the position you are seeking may also be included. You may also want to include pastimes and interests that are relevant.

8. What not to include

You don't need to mention whether or not you have a driving licence, nor how many children you have, unless it is relevant to the job. Nor should you include references. That can come later, once you are offered the job.

CV Worksheet

Name
Address
Telephone
Email

Profile

....
....
....

Key skills or achievements (depending on CV format)

Career history

Company   Dates
Job title
Scope

Achievements

....
....

Company   Dates

Job title

Scope

WRITING AN EFFECTIVE CV

Achievements

Company   Dates

Job title

Scope

Achievements

Education

Dates	Institution	Subjects	Grade

Additional Information (Hobbies, Interests, etc.)

CV Dos

- Keep it simple, clear and easy to read;
- Target the CV to the job applied for;
- Use short, concise sentences;
- Start with the first draft and expect to do several revisions;
- Start with the most important information at the beginning;
- Focus on your special abilities;
- Put your achievement statements in order – most relevant first;
- Quantify the results of your achievements where possible;
- Tell the truth;
- Be consistent in punctuation and capitalisation;
- Check your spelling;
- Use past tense for all achievements: this emphasises completion;
- Start every sentence with an action verb;
- Make it visually appealing;
- Keep it to one or two pages maximum;
- Have it critiqued and proofread by others;
- Avoid unusual fonts and colours or shading. Arial or Times Roman at 11/12 points size is best. CVs are often scanned, faxed or copied.

CV Don'ts

■ Don't include information that is not relevant to your ability to perform the job, for example:

Health, height, weight, or marital status;
References or the words 'References can be supplied upon request';
Salary history or requirements;
Reasons for leaving previous position(s).

■ Don't leave gaps between employment dates without stating a good reason for the gap.
■ Don't be modest (use achievement statements).
■ Don't use the phrase 'responsible for...' (refer to the action word list).
■ Don't include negative information.
■ Don't use abbreviations (make it a formal document).
■ Don't include your photograph unless required to do so.
■ Don't use business-specific jargon or complicated technical sentences unless it is destined for a technical audience.
■ Don't write long sentences or paragraphs of prose.
■ Don't use colours or complicated fonts.
■ Don't use tables or graphics unless you are sending your CV as a pdf. These can distort when opened on other computers or in different packages.

CV Templates
1. Achievement focused CV

Name
Address Postcode
Home Telephone Mobile Email

Spend two or three lines summarising your role, experience, skills and strengths. Avoid too many adjectives and clichés like 'good communicator' – try something more specific like 'accomplished public speaker', 'proficient mentor', 'at ease in making presentations'. Keep font sizes large throughout.

Achievements
■ Bulleted list of four or five major achievements. Keep each achievement to two lines if possible, certainly no more than three.

■ These can be achievements at work or in your private life, as long as they show an aspect of your personality which is relevant to your application.

■ This is the part of the page which catches the reader's eye first. Make sure it grabs their attention.

Key Skills
■ Bulleted list of four or five major skills. These might include:
■ Systems and products in which you are experienced;
■ Fields of work in which you excel;
■ Any expertise that makes you stand out.

Be sure you can prove your skills. Avoid general statements like 'ambitious' or 'energetic' – unless you clearly come across as such at interview.

Career History
You only need to include jobs during the last 5–10 years, or jobs that were of particular significance. Include start and end years. Don't include months unless in the last three years.

Dates | Position | Employer
■ Summarise your principle tasks and responsibilities. If appropriate, include the size of budget and number of team members/staff.

■ Then list your achievement statements using a bulleted list if possible (see page 72). You want the reader to get a sense of your main strengths.

■ Make sure your achievement statements demonstrate clear evidence of your key skills.

■ Don't put too much in. Remember, your CV is your tool to get you to interview. It has to jump out at the reader. Don't risk boring them.

■ If you are trying to sell yourself on the basis of a job you had earlier in your career, spend more time describing what you did there.

Education
Dates and name of institution, type of qualification (degree, GNVQ, Alevels, etc.) and subjects if relevant. Don't give irrelevant information – if you didn't finish a course, don't mention it. If you are over 50 with postgraduate degrees, don't list your O levels

Training
List any relevant courses that you have been on (with dates and name of the training provider). If there are too many, include them on a separate sheet as an appendix.

Professional Bodies
List any professional bodies, societies, interest groups, etc. that you belong to.

Publications
If you have published anything which is relevant to your job application, include it here. If there are too many, include them on a separate sheet as an appendix.

Interests and hobbies

Personal information

Give your date of birth and any relevant information that you feel will help your case. You don't need to include your marital status etc. unless you want to.

Dos and Don'ts:
Do decide whether an achievements based CV is right for you and the job you're applying for .
Do keep your CV down to 2 pages.
Do make your CV look attractive. Play around with font sizes and layouts.
Do keep your CV in black type. CVs are usually copied by recruiters so don't do anything that might make the copies come out badly.

Don't include references. That will come later, if your application goes forward to a later stage.
Don't include salary. That will come later, when you're negotiating the job.
Don't include too much information. When a recruiter is sorting five hundred CVs into Yes, No and Maybe piles, anything that is too much trouble to read is bound to be rejected.
Don't undersell yourself, or oversell yourself. Be accurate, focused and positive.
Don't put down anything that is untrue or that you cannot support at an interview.

2. Skills focused CV

Name
Address Postcode
Home Telephone Mobile Email

Spend two or three lines summarising your role, experience, skills and strengths. Avoid too many adjectives and clichés like 'good communicator' – try something more specific like 'accomplished public speaker', 'proficient mentor', 'at ease in making presentations'. Keep font sizes large throughout.

Key skills
- Bulleted list of four or five major skills. These might include:
- Systems and products in which you are experienced;
- Fields of work in which you excel;
- Any expertise that makes you stand out.

Be sure you can prove your skills. Avoid general statements like 'ambitious' or 'energetic' – unless you clearly come across as such at interview.

This is the part of the page which catches the reader's eye first. Make sure it grabs their attention.

Career history
You only need to include jobs during the last 5–10 years, or jobs that were of particular significance. Include start and end years. Don't include months unless in the last three years.

Dates | Position | Employer
- Summarise your principal tasks, responsibilities and competencies.

- Use a bulleted list if possible. You want the reader to get a sense of your main strengths.

- If appropriate, include the size of budget and number of team members/staff you were responsible for.

- Then list your achievement statements using a bulleted list if possible (see page 72). You want the reader to get a sense of your main strengths.

- Make sure your achievement statements demonstrate clear evidence of your key skills.

- Don't put too much in. Remember, your CV is your tool to get you to interview. It has to jump out at the reader. Don't risk boring them.

- If you are trying to sell yourself on the basis of a job you had earlier in your career, spend more time describing what you did there.

Early career history

List briefly jobs you had when you were younger, including years, job title and company. Keep it short. If an earlier job was of particular significance, include it in the section above.

Education

Dates and name of institution, type of qualification (degree, GNVQ, Alevels, etc.) and subjects if relevant. Don't give irrelevant information – if you didn't finish a course, don't mention it. If you are over 50 with postgraduate degrees, don't list your Olevels

Training

List any relevant courses that you have been on (with dates and name of the training provider). If there are too many, include on a separate sheet as an appendix.

Professional bodies

List any professional bodies, societies, interest groups, etc. that you belong to.

Publications

If you have published anything which is relevant to your job application, include it here. If there are too many, include them on a separate sheet as an appendix.

Interests and hobbies

Personal information

Give your date of birth and any relevant information that you feel will help your case. You don't need to include your marital status etc. unless you want to.

Dos and Don'ts:

Do decide whether a skills based CV is right for you and the job you're applying for.

Do keep your CV down to two pages if at all possible. Certainly no more than three.

Do make your CV look attractive. Play around with font sizes and layouts.

Do keep your CV in black type. CVs are usually copied by recruiters so don't do anything that might make the copies come out badly.

Don't include references. That will come later, if your application goes forward to a later stage.

Don't include salary. That will come later, when you're negotiating the job.

Don't include too much information. When a recruiter is sorting five hundred CVs into Yes, No and Maybe piles, anything that is too much trouble to read is bound to be rejected.

Don't undersell yourself, or oversell yourself. Be accurate, focused and positive.

Don't put down anything that is untrue or that you cannot support at an interview.

3. Functional CV

Name
Address Postcode
Home Telephone Mobile Email

Spend two or three lines summarising your role, experience, skills and strengths. Avoid too many adjectives and clichés like 'good communicator' – try something more specific like 'accomplished public speaker', 'proficient mentor', 'at ease in making presentations'. Keep font sizes large throughout.

Key skills and expertise
Bulleted list of four or five major skills. These might include:

■ Systems and products in which you are experienced;
■ Fields of work in which you excel;
■ Type and range of projects you have worked on;
■ Any expertise that makes you stand out.

Be sure you can prove your skills. Avoid general statements like 'ambitious' or 'energetic' unless you clearly come across as such at interview.

■ This is the part of the page which catches the reader's eye first. Make sure it grabs their attention.

Areas of expertise
■ Write headings for the key areas of expertise you have highlighted above.

■ Under each heading give specific examples of your successes in these areas. For example:

People management and leadership
■ Example A;   ■ Example B;   ■ Example C.

■ List them in achievement statement format.

■ You want the reader to get a sense of your main strengths.

■ If appropriate, include the scope of activities such as the size of budget and number of team members/staff you were responsible for.

■ Make sure your achievement statements demonstrate positive measurable outcomes (e.g. expressed in £, $, %, value added for customers) and clear evidence of your key expertise or skills.

■ Don't put too much in. Remember, your CV is your tool to get you to interview. It has to jump out at the reader. Don't risk boring them.

■ If you are trying to sell yourself on the basis of a job you had earlier in your career, spend more time describing what you did there.

Career history

List your career history briefly to give an account of your career progression. For example:

Start Year–Finish Year	Role	Company Name
Start Year–Finish Year	Role	Company Name
Start Year–Finish Year	Role	Company Name

Training

List any relevant courses that you have been on (with dates and name of the training provider). If there are too many, include on a separate sheet as an appendix.

Education

Dates and name of institution, type of qualification (degree, GNVQ, Alevels, etc.) and subjects if relevant. Don't give irrelevant information – if you didn't finish a course, don't mention it. If you are over 50 with postgraduate degrees, don't list your Olevels

Professional bodies

List any professional bodies, societies, interest groups, etc. that you belong to.

Publications

If you have published anything which is relevant to your job application, include it here. If there are too many, include on a separate sheet as an appendix.

Interests and hobbies

Personal information

Give your date of birth and any relevant information that you feel will help your case. You don't need to include your marital status etc. unless you want to.

Dos and Don'ts:

Do decide whether a functional CV is right for you and the job you're applying for.

Do keep your CV down to two pages if at all possible. Certainly no more than three.

Do make your CV look attractive. Play around with font sizes and layouts.

Do keep your CV in black type. CVs are usually copied by recruiters so don't do anything that might make the copies come out badly.

Don't include references. That will come later, if your application goes forward to a later stage.

Don't include salary. That will come later, when you're negotiating the job.

Don't include too much information. When a recruiter is sorting five hundred CVs into Yes, No and Maybe piles, anything that is too much trouble to read is bound to be rejected.

Don't undersell yourself, or oversell yourself. Be accurate, focused and positive.

Don't put down anything that is untrue or that you cannot support at an interview.

7. Making best use of recruitment consultants

In a recession, when jobs are scarce and you can't find a similar position to your previous role, it is quite likely you will find yourself applying for jobs you know you can do but have never done before, or into counter cyclical sectors where you know you can work but have never previously worked. This doesn't just apply to sectors where the downturn has been most severe, like finance or the automotive industry. We don't know where a recession will strike next; all sectors are equally vulnerable. Even insolvency practitioners, who may find themselves hit by changes in the law, or by increased competition from other professional service firms may suffer!

And so you may need to make a career change. If so, it is likely you may find yourself frustrated by recruitment consultants who do not take you seriously. Instead of helping you to make the change they will look at your CV and tell you that you don't have the relevant experience.

This response, repeated three or four times, is often enough to discourage you from progressing any further.

There are two things going on here. The first is that you are not marketing yourself effectively into your new career. You may have a good CV, but it portrays you as someone who is successful in the field of work you are trying to get away from. It doesn't necessarily make out a convincing case to support your move into your new field.

The second is that you are talking to the wrong people! Most recruitment consultants specialise in specific industries. They are engaged by employers to fill particular vacancies. They won't have many vacancies on their books during a recession and they will be looking for good fits; they are unlikely to go out and search for a job for you which matches your aspirations.

Even if you go to a recruiter who specialises directly in the field that you want to enter, the chances are that they will not encourage you. In a difficult employment climate, unless your CV directly markets you into the role you want, and it is clear to them that they will have no trouble placing you into one of the vacancies on their books, they will almost certainly relegate you to the bottom of the pile and concentrate on those candidates who appear to be better qualified for the post.

As we have already said, the probability is that you will not get the first job of your new career through a recruitment consultant or agency. In fact most jobs come about through word of mouth. According to Robert S. Gardella of Harvard Business School, between 65 and 70 per cent of jobs come through networking. Career guru John Lees estimates that only 20–30 per cent of vacancies are published. In our experience a significant number of jobs come through well-targeted direct approaches to companies to whom you clearly have something offer.

However, even though networking is the most likely route for you to get a job in a recession, you can't afford to overlook any avenue. You will need to deal with recruiters. So how will you do it? Let's take a look at the role of recruiters and see how you can utilise them to maximum advantage.

Methods of recruitment

There are three main types of recruitment: selection, search and contingency.

Selection

This is when the recruitment agency advertises to attract suitable candidates and might run assessment centres before creating a short list of suitable people for the employer to interview. This is almost always an exclusive arrangement between the employer and one recruitment agency. The employer, who is the agency's client, pays part of the fee at the outset and part when the job is offered to a successful candidate.

Search

Search is more popularly known as 'headhunting'. The recruiter will work to a brief from the employer to identify a candidate who is currently in work. Rather than advertising the recruiter will research and network to get names of potential candidates to approach. The point about this sort of recruitment is that the employer is looking for someone senior or specialised, and assumes that the person they want will be waiting for an approach rather than putting themselves forward in the job market. The important thing to understand is that genuine head-hunters find you, not the other way round.

Search and selection is often done by the same companies, and sometimes for the same brief.

Contingency

This covers most recruitment. Candidates submit their CV to register with an agency, and clients submit recruitment briefs. The agency acts like a matchmaker, submitting appropriate CVs to clients to consider. The client carries out all further selection activity. A fee is earned only if a placement is made.

Recruiters often advertise on their own behalf using what is known as a 'menu'. These are a selection of jobs currently being recruited for, aimed at informing people about the type of role the agency handles and encouraging registration.

How recruiters operate

Although it is you who is being recruited it's the employer that pays the recruitment fee. You pay nothing. This obviously encourages candidates to register with or respond to recruiters. The problem is that, since you do not bring any money to the table, recruiters can easily lose interest in you if they feel they are unlikely to place you and hence earn a fee from the employer. Their objective is to fill vacancies, not to get you a job.

To make things worse, contingency recruiters compete against each other for candidates and assignments. But they don't receive any money until a placement is made. Unlike search and selection recruiters they don't get an intial fee from the employer when they take on a brief. However, once a contingency recruiter has submitted your CV to an employer, they will earn the fee if the company decides to employ you. Nobody else can. So you may find yourself under quite a bit of pressure to send your details in and give permission for the agency to send them out to potential employers. Don't allow yourself to be pushed into this if you are not ready.

Some recruiters rewrite CVs into a house style, often because clients want to be able to compare candidates for a single job quickly and easily. This is acceptable as long as it is accurate. But you do need to keep control of this process. Otherwise you may find that you are trying to network yourself into a meeting with a particular company, only to discover that they have already seen a poorly reworked version of your CV sent in by a recruiter. This can ruin your chances. So make sure that your recruitment consultant shows you the finished version of the CV they intend to circulate, and make your views known if you are not happy. It is a good idea to take a copy of your original CV to any company that the recruiter introduces you to and leave it with the interviewer if you are interested in taking things further with them.

Recruiters should send notes with the CV outlining your personality, relevant experience and why they are submitting you. They should also give the employer information about your salary, notice-period, availability, etc.

How recruiters advertise

There are two ways by which recruiters advertise. The process is similar for print media and the internet.

The first is known as a menu advertisement. In this case the recruitment agency lists out a range of positions for which they are seeking to attract candidates. They don't name employers, they just give summaries of the job descriptions. The idea is to demonstrate their expertise in a particular sector, or for a particular type of job and to convince you that they have so many positions available that you just don't need to go anywhere else! The recruiter pays for these advertisements themselves.

The other type of recruiter advert is known as client paid advertising. As the name suggests, the employer is paying for this and they will be advertising just one or two vacancies that they have. The advertisement may or may not include the employer's name and details. The aim is to generate interest in the specific positions. However, if you respond to one of these adverts and the employer decides they do not want to take things further with you, you may find that the recruiter will approach you with details of other vacancies that they have.

Advertising on the internet offers very wide coverage and tends to attract vast numbers of people from outside the specialisation, especially when generalist boards are used, such as Monster or TotalJobs. You need to bear this in mind when applying for jobs that you have seen online. It is very difficult for suitable candidates to get noticed and you will be relying on the recruiter's ability to sift and sort applicants properly. For this reason you should treat online advertising with caution and not spend too long applying for jobs that you don't want, or don't stand a reasonable chance of getting.

Adverts in the national press are expensive and are often only used for senior management appointments or where the employer wants to ensure they are reaching as wide an audience as possible. Selection recruiters often use the national press as it is a good way to secure plenty of applications.

What can recruiters do for you?
If a recruiter feels they can earn a fee through you they can be helpful. But if not, you are unlikely to find the relationship very productive. Nevertheless, even though networking remains the most likely route to getting a job, agencies still handle a good number of opportunities and should be taken seriously as a source of opportunities.

Many employers announce vacancies through recruiters only, and recruiters, particularly sector specialists, often have strong contacts giving them access to potential employers through speculative approaches. In addition, many companies give their preferred recruiter an open brief to find suitable talent.

The first thing most contingency recruiters will do when a brief arrives is a database search of existing candidates. This is a quick and easy way to identify any past candidates who may be suitable and interested, without spending money on advertising.

A good recruiter will interview you face to face before registering you or putting you up for a job. They should use the meeting to gain an understanding of your career background and objectives, which they will attempt to match to the requirements of their clients. They will then talk to you about any assignments that appear to offer a potential fit. If they do not suggest any opportunities you can assume they have nothing that is right for you. Try to assess if this is because you are not presenting yourself as their normal type of client or they just don't have something for you at the time. If it's the former, you may need to think about whether you should be positioning yourself differently, or going to a different agency.

Recruiters will always look for an easy route to make a placement. They operate in an extremely competitive market place and all the more so in a recession because of the limited number of vacancies available. They will concentrate on candidates who look likely to be suitable for their clients rather than people who will demand more time and effort to place. Which takes us back to what we said earlier on. If you are making a career change your CV really does need to market you into your new role. Unless it does, you are likely to find the recruitment consultant route very unproductive.

If you are submitted for a position, the recruiter clearly wants you to succeed. They should help you as much as they can with background information and you shouldn't shy away from asking them as much as you can. They might even conduct a mock interview with you. But you will still need to do your own research. Never rely on a recruiter to give you all the background information you need.

Choosing a recruiter

As with all things, a trusted recommendation is worth more than any amount of advertising. Speak to your friends and contacts about which recruiters they have used and whether or not they would recommend them.

In the absence of a recommendation, check the specialist trade press. Regular advertisers can be assumed to have access to the right type of opportunities for you. However, you won't know about the quality of the service so be sure to ask the right questions before deciding to register.

Signs of expertise are:
- Consultants with previous experience working in the industry;
- Regular ads for jobs in your field, especially branded ads;
- Understanding of technical subtleties in your area of work;
- An impressive client list.

For added security, look for a membership of one of the trade associations. They will have a strict code of conduct to which members are expected to adhere.

You need to manage your recruiter carefully so it is important not to register with too many agencies. Don't be fooled into thinking that quantity is better than quality. If agencies with whom you do not have a well managed relationship are able to rewrite and distribute your CV without your knowledge then you are just storing up trouble for yourself.

There is an exception to the above. The IT sector, particularly contracting, works on skills profile almost to the exclusion of any other characteristic and the need for the recruiter to understand your personality is less important. It is therefore recommended that you approach a larger number of agencies as any one might be handling an assignment requiring your background. In essence, where you are trading on skills, past work experience and qualifications only, spread the net wide; where you are looking for a strong fit and career development with a company be more focused.

Managing your recruiter

Make sure your recruiter feels they can earn a fee from you! Present yourself well, with a clear objective, a good CV and a strong interview technique. Take your meeting with the recruiter as seriously as your job interviews, and then they'll know you mean business! Make sure your CV is easy to read and shows clearly what you have to offer. Recruiters read many CVs each week. The ones they take note of are the ones that instantly appeal to them – the ones that lead them to say 'I can place this person'.

If recruiters don't have opportunities for you, or if they can't get you to engage with the vacancies they have, they will lose interest in you. So make sure that they fully understand your requirements and show enthusiasm for whatever they do put your way, even if the job doesn't really excite you all that much. Who knows, the next vacancy they put in front of you might be the one you have waited for all your life!

But do make sure they always keep you updated with what they are doing. A good recruiter will never send a CV to a prospective employer without first asking your permission and giving you a good comprehensive briefing.

When a recruiter does brief you about a vacancy make sure to ask all the important questions about:

■ The company history, direction, strategy and structure;

■ The job title, salary, team structure, role and other roles in the team;

■ Minimum requirements for the position and as much information about the line manager and recruitment process as possible.

Keep in regular contact with your recruiters. Don't pester them, but make sure that you keep yourself on their radar. Contact them every couple of weeks or so. And of course, make sure they treat you with respect and demonstrate their commitment to confidentiality.

Don't fall into the trap of going for interviews 'for practice'. Many consultants persuade people to go for interviews on this basis but it is a myth. There are two reasons for going to an interview:

1.   *Because you are keen on the job or*
2.   *Because you see it as a networking opportunity.*

If you are not interested in meeting the person you will fail to perform and therefore you will fail to impress.

Keep records of your contact with recruiters and of the opportunities they put you way. Your logs should look something like this:

Recruiter record sheet

Agency	Consultant	Contact details	Source	First contact date	Interview date/form	Latest contact/ notes

Opportunities through recruiters

Agency	Company/ position	CV submitted	Interview 1	Interview 2	Interview 2

8. Making speculative approaches 1 – doing your research

Speculative approaches

Sometimes you will know that what you offer is exactly right for a particular company and, try as you might, you have been unable to effect a connection through your networks. In these cases the only thing left to you is approach the company directly, without an introduction, using what we call a speculative approach.

There are two parts to a speculative application. First of all you need to research the company well, to make sure that you really do fit the bill as far as they are concerned. Your research also needs to lead you to discover who you should be approaching in the company, and what their contact details are.

Secondly, you need to make the right approach to them, whether this is by letter, email or phone. But do your research first!

In this chapter we will look at how to do good research. Then in the next chapter we will turn to how to make the right approach.

Researching companies before making a speculative approach

Good research increases your chances of getting the right job, rather than just any job. But good research takes time and is only of any use if you take action based on what you have learned from your research. Good research will allow you to:

■ Be proactive in your job search. You will be able to spot and to create opportunities for yourself, rather than waiting for them to come to you.

■ Find out about unfamiliar industries and sectors that may be suitable for you to move into if the recession has closed off all opportunities in your current sector.

■ Discover companies that match your ideal target, that have a culture that you want to work in, that are based in the location you want to be and that will enable you to do the things you want to do.

■ Have the information you need to write a well targeted and relevant application to the company.

■ Improve your networking skills because you will have more relevant information on the topic of conversation.

■ Perform better at interviews. Not only will you will be able to demonstrate knowledge of the company; the fact that you have taken an interest by carrying out detailed research will count in your favour.

Most importantly, in the current economic climate, good research will help you identify which companies are likely to survive, and which are on the point of going under. Companies that are riding the recession successfully are likely to be interested in picking up the talent coming onto the market. Equally there is absolutely no point in your spending time writing to companies that are likely to go bust. The chances of them giving you a job are zilch.

Preparing for research

Before you start, make a list of what you want to know. This might include:

- Information on sector trends and forecasts;
- The names of companies in the sector;
- Names and contact details of the key decision makers in a company;
- Information on a company's products and services;
- Company financials;
- Recent news stories about a company.

Consider the places to access this information. Some of this information will be available on the internet, other information might only be available by networking with the right people. Alert Data is a particularly useful subscription database to use during your research.

Public libraries are a good research resource, particularly business and reference libraries. They will have directories, journals and professional publications as well as newspapers and reference books. They may also have access to online resources that otherwise require a subscription. As well as your local library, check out the local Business School or University library.

Questions to ask during research
Researching industries

Who are the major players (key companies) in this industry?
What is the size and shape of this industry?
What are the current economic effects such as growth or decline of demand?
What are the regulatory bodies in charge of this industry?

Will government initiatives create or decrease job opportunities?
Are there reports on the industry put out by the responsible government department?
What is the global impact on this industry?
What are the critical success factors and the outside influences that can affect the industry?
Are there any recent articles in the press discussing the industry?
Is there an industry association or professional body that could give you information?

Researching companies

What exactly does the company do? What is the full range of products or services?
How is it structured? Is it private or public? Is there an overseas parent? Are there subsidiaries? Who are the major shareholders?
What are the facts around the company? Size? Turnover? Number of employees? Financials? Profitability? Market share?
What does the history tell you regarding mergers and buyouts?
Who are the senior people and who is likely to make a decision about the job opportunities in your field?
What can you discover about the business plans, mission statement and marketing approach of the company?
Who are the main competitors?
How does the culture of the company affect employment – values, approaches to career development, training and recruitment?

9. Making speculative approaches 2 – writing speculative letters

It may have surprised you to learn that most jobs are never advertised, but if you think about it for a moment it makes sense. Advertising is expensive and the employer knows nothing about the people who reply to the advert besides what their CVs reveal. In contrast if they try to recruit by word of mouth employers will reach candidates who either they know themselves or have been introduced by someone they trust. Therefore, for most employers, advertising is a method of last resort.

So if most jobs are not advertised then it is well worth you writing a well-crafted speculative letter to the companies you are targeting. They may well have vacancies that you just don't know about, because you have not seen an advert.

The purpose of a speculative letter is to stimulate the recipient's interest in you. So it needs to be well written and sell you strongly. And it needs to be directed not just to the right company, but to the right person in the company.

Who to write to

To have the greatest impact your speculative letters need to be carefully targeted to the right person, the one who will make the decision to hire. This might be the head of a department or a board member, depending on the size of the company. When you do your research this is one of the things you should try to find out. Don't write speculatively to human resources or personnel, unless of course you want to work in that department.

Your letter

Your letter should be no longer than a page and a half. Every single word is important, so take your time and make sure you get it right.

As a general rule, do not send your CV at this stage. Your aim is to get a meeting at which they can learn more about you. Sending the CV can lead to rejection before you have the chance to find out their real needs. The following pointers are important in writing a good speculative letter:

1. Personalise it

Make sure you know the name and title of the the person to whom you are writing – don't write Dear Sir/Madam. Do check your spelling – particularly of the addressee's name, and the address, before you mail a letter. Don't rely on the accuracy of directories or mailing lists which are often out of date almost as soon as they are compiled.

The best way to make sure that you are using accurate information is to phone each of your target companies and ask them to confirm the details.

2. Attract the reader's attention

A good sales letter starts by attracting the reader's attention. We call the first statement you make a hook. This statement is likely to be something about them, or the company. It should not be about you. You can obtain your hook from the annual report, from press reports, from looking in research material. Or you may be able to get information on the person to whom you're writing which you can use for an attention grabbing introduction. Good places to look for this are on LinkedIn, Facebook and Google. Some examples of hooks, or opening statements are:

'I read with interest of ABC Company's plan to open a new distribution facility in Woking. Such a facility will no doubt need people with expertise in …';

'The recently announced government strategy to increase the compliance of … will no doubt put additional pressure on your legal department';

'I saw your profile on LinkedIn and realised that we have a mutual contact in...'.

Don't start with:
'I am an experienced account manager';
'I would be interested in working for your company'
or anything else like that. You will simply turn them off before they read the rest of the letter.

3. Get them interested in what you have to say

The next stage is to interest them in what you have to offer. This means putting yourself in their shoes and asking yourself what you would want to read in a letter from a candidate, if you were them. For example:

'In a recession cash flow is king and a good credit controller can make all the difference to a company's revenues';

'The pressures on your sales team must be even greater in the current climate and those who can keep a cool head are most likely to succeed'.

Next you need to back up these statements with evidence about yourself and your achievements. It helps if you can do so in such a way that it reads brightly and cheerfully, so that you can maintain the reader's interest. Be careful to avoid anything that may be construed as a negative.

Explain your achievements and experience so that they are seen to be relevant to the organisation that you are approaching and show how your experience fits with their culture and their operation. Select from your achievements the best two or three, which most closely match your perception of the needs of the company, and include them in your letter.

4. A positive close

Finish the letter on a positive statement, which shows you are expecting a favourable reaction:

'I would appreciate the opportunity to meet with you to discuss in more detail my background in relation to your needs';

'I will call you in a few days to establish your level of interest in my background'.

Follow up within three or four days of sending the letter. If you get a positive response arrange a meeting to discuss their needs further. If you are rejected thank them for the response and try to set up a network meeting. If you cannot get a response, make sure the letter was received and again try for a networking meeting.

5. Wording

The most effective words are the ones you use normally. Be concise so you don't slow down the reader. Be positive and use powerful, active words. Avoid jargon, even the company's own jargon!

Sentences should be long enough to express a complete thought, but short sentences are easier to read and make sure you get to the point!

Shorter paragraphs also have power. If a paragraph is too long your reader may get lost in the text. State your main idea in the opening sentence and have one idea per paragraph, as your sentences should connect. Make sure you keep the same verb tense.

Make sure you proofread your letter again and again ... a single mistake may be fatal!

6. Test your letters

First reread what you have written out loud to hear how it comes across. You can avoid repetitions and bulky sentences this way. If you stumble in reading it, your sentences may be too long or complicated.

Ask, *'So what?'* about every point you make. If you cannot see a reason to be interested in your services, you need to rewrite your points so they have more impact and clearer benefits for the reader.

Next ask a third party to review to see if they get the same message you intended. Test your letter on a small sample. If the response is positive then continue. If the response is negative, then you need to revise your letter. In any event you do not want to send out too many letters at one time as you need time to effectively follow them up and do further research.

Example speculative letter

The letter on page 111 is thorough enough to send without a CV. You can tailor it to your circumstances.

24 Rose Lane
Woking
Surrey
GU13 4NU

Ms Sally Fookes
General Manager
Redfield Engineering
60 Queens Road
Southampton
Hants SO43 1HU
(Date)

Dear Ms Fookes

Hook
Five years ago, most engineering consultancies were overloaded with projects and clients. Today the competitive global economy has changed the shape of the market. This demands a fresh approach to ensure maintenance and growth of the business.

Relevant information
As Marketing Manager for Western Services Ltd, I was responsible for new business development strategies, advertising and public relations. I was also the marketing strategist for two subsidiaries. Prior to this I had established the joint venture with Smiths Enterprises – another market leader, which currently has a turnover in excess of £14 million.

I have proven expertise in turning around market declines by implementing creative and demanding plans which lead to significant increase in market share. On several occasions my efforts have been rewarded with industry recognition through awards.

Before joining Western, I was Marketing Manager for CXS. There I was the key player in the new business start up: setting the strategy, instigating operating procedures and recruiting and leading the management team. This team is still in place and producing consistently healthy results.

Positive close
Given my experience and the needs of Redfield Engineering in the current climate, I would welcome the opportunity to discuss our mutual interest in marketing. If I may, I will call you within the next ten days to see when we can meet.

Yours sincerely

Signature

(Name)

10. Cold calling

A carefully prepared and well-delivered cold call can be extremely effective – if you get through to the right person. But most of us find the idea uncomfortable and shy away from it. So what can you do to feel more comfortable about cold calling and include it as part of your arsenal?

Cold calling has a number of advantages:

■ Telephoning is quicker than writing and much more personal. If you research and plan well you can make dozens of fact-finding and appointment-producing telephone calls in a day.

■ You can get in touch directly with decision makers (although of course this is not guaranteed).

■ People tend to be much warmer in meetings if they have had a phone conversation first. They feel they already know you a little bit, their initial reserve and caution is tempered somewhat.

■ It is much easier to make an appointment by phone than by letter or email.

How to cold call
1. Define your target list
This is no different from defining the list of people to whom you write speculative letters. Ideally you will be calling the person who will make the decision to hire. The only difference this time is that you will probably have to talk to someone else first – their 'gatekeeper' – before you can raise them on the phone. So when you do your research, try to

find out the name of their PA or secretary, it will benefit you if you can form a relationship with them first.

As with letters, don't cold call human resources or personnel, unless that is the department that you want to work in. Be tenacious and, if necessary, call back a number of times in order to speak to your target (try not to leave your name and telephone number – unless they know you they are unlikely to return your call, and it stops you ringing them again).

2. Decide on your objective

Before you pick up the telephone, clarify what you aim to achieve in the next five minutes. Ideally this is to set up a firm date and time for a meeting but this may not be so easy. So make your goal to set up a meeting, but map out some intermediate stages that you can accomplish in a phone call in case you cannot achieve your goal. For example, you might get them to agree to look at your CV, or give you the name of someone else in the company who you should be talking to. If you cannot achieve your goal of getting a meeting the important thing is to keep your lines of communication open.

3. Scripting your conversations

You will find it useful to write yourself a script before making your first call. This involves carefully choosing words, phrases and sentences, weaving them together into a coherent form and planning how to use them for maximum effect. Try to run your script past someone you know to get their reaction before using it for the first time.

Make sure that you use your script as a prompt, but don't read it word for word otherwise you are likely to come across as dull and lifeless. This will be particularly true once you have read it a few times and are becoming bored with it.

The first phone call takes longest to prepare. The more calls you make, the sharper your skills become. In addition, the better your planning, the more likely you are to make your calls confidently and persuasively. Your telephone conversation will normally only last two to three minutes, so it is important that you use the time well and get to the crux of the conversation as efficiently as you can.

Firstly prepare your opening pitch, which should dispose of any uncertainty in the mind of the person you are calling about:

- Why you have rung;
- Why they should talk to you;
- Why you have rung them in particular.

The opening of your phone call needs to establish efficient rapport to keep the caller on the line and to create interest in what you have to say. Remember that the person you have just rung was not expecting your call, is likely to be busy and is probably very tempted to hang up on you or to pass the call back to her secretary. So make sure that they know why you are calling and that they are willing to talk to you. Don't open by asking how they are, or how their weekend was, or passing your opinion on the weather. These are the sorts of things that frustrate the recipients of cold calls, they are likely to view them as a distraction or, even worse, an irritation.

Move quickly to the reason for your call. This may be a referral from someone, in which case mention their name, or it may be because you are researching something.

If at any time you sense that they want to end the call, don't impede them. Have a closing request lined up which asks, for example, whether you can drop them an email to explain why you are calling, or perhaps if there is a better time for you to call them back.

But if you can establish a rapport, if the conversation is flowing relatively well, then move as speedily as you can to explain the link between your background and their needs. For example, you may have:

■ Relevant industry experience or qualifications;
■ Relevant functional experience or training;
■ Relevant exposure to their kind of problems.

In each case, be specific. Don't waffle. If you feel you still have time in the call to add further information or to demonstrate why you are worth seeing, refer to your script and tell them:

■ What you know about their company;
■ What you see as a possible role for yourself in their company;
■ About your achievements and credentials.

Next, try to ask questions so that you can clarify their needs. Create dialogue. Listen. Be positive. End the call on a positive note.

4. Plan and rehearse

You probably know from your own experience, and in any event research has demonstrated, that when you make a phone call, even though the recipient cannot see you, they can detect your mood. So prepare yourself mentally to ensure that you project a warm, positive and self-assured image. Your smile can be heard on the telephone! If you smile when you speak over the phone, you sound more confident, friendly and enthusiastic.

Make a series of calls in a row, without waiting too long in between. You will become more fluent and relaxed as you make the calls. Repeated calls will allow you to project greater confidence. Many people stand when they cold call; it centres your body, increasing your confidence and having a positive effect on your tone of voice.

5. Ask for the meeting

Don't leave it to them to suggest a meeting. It probably won't happen. Use your judgement about timing the question and take the plunge. It is better to be too early than too late. You should attempt to move to this stage as soon as you get a clear signal that they are interested in you. Some lines that you can use to move the conversation towards agreeing a meeting are:

'... yes, I would like to see what you have.'
'... tell me about your experience with ABC Co.'
'... when would you be available?'

The tone of voice will very often indicate that they are interested.

If a meeting is not to be, see if you can get some introductions to other key people in the company or sector.

Always remember to thank the person you have spoken to, irrespective of the outcome.

Traps and pitfalls

Avoid the following:

■ Starting with excuses or being negative at the start – 'I'm sorry to bother you';

■ 'I know you don't have any vacancies but ...';

■ Expecting them to control the call (they don't know your objectives);

■ Wasting time with small talk (first impressions are crucial; time is precious);

■ Talking too much (try to ask questions and get them talking);

■ Using closed questions that will result in yes or no answers – it is very hard to move the conversation forward from this point;

■ Talking for too long: they are busy so end the call when a meeting is agreed or earlier if you sense that is what they are trying to do.

Handling objections

It is perfectly natural for people to raise objections during cold calls, as they will try to make sure that you are not wasting their time. The most important aid in dealing with objections is to have the right attitude towards them. They are not obstacles – but opportunities to:

■ Listen more carefully to their needs;
■ Analyse what they want in more detail;
■ Give them information;
■ Explain your background with more examples;
■ Convince them how you can be of benefit to the company.

Remember, every objection that they raise indicates that they have been paying attention to you. So treat objections as opportunities and build on them. A good technique for overcoming objections is to create common ground:

■ Listen: do not interrupt but take notes of what they are saying so that you respond when your turn comes to talk.

■ Agree: recognise they are valued objections.

■ Clarify: do not pounce back, but try to understand what they are saying.

■ Ask questions, 'So the position is …'.

■ Summarise: do not argue, but get your contact to accept that you have a good point.

■ Avoid the word 'but': the more positive word 'and' can work just as well.

Example objections

Objection 'You sound too senior for us.'
Reply 'It's the quality and content of the work that appeals to me, not the job title or status in the company.'

Objection 'We only recruit people with accounting degrees.'
Reply 'I have exactly the work experience required by the role.'
Or
'Could you tell me which part of the degree applies to the role? I have taken several accounting courses that will have covered most aspects of the degree.'

Objection 'You've had global responsibilities – we're much smaller.'
Reply 'My work was only in one department of that company, which was the same size and scope as this company.'
Or
'I actually prefer smaller organisations. That's one of the main reasons I was interested in what you have to offer.'

Objection 'We don't have any opportunities at the moment.'
Reply 'Could you give me some idea of the number of vacancies you have had in the last year?'
Or

'Do you anticipate any potential opportunities for someon
the future as I am very interested in your company?'

Objection 'We need someone with a background in this industry.'
Reply 'Industry experience can be invaluable, but knowledge and
exposure to complex projects in other industries can be equally helpful.
I am very flexible and adapt quickly to new environments'
Or
'I have experience in a number of different industries and have always
made the transition well, bringing the best of the industries I have left
with me. I have always enjoyed the challenge.'

Points to remember

■ Catch your target's interest at the start – within 20 seconds most
people will decide who you are, what you really want, and whether or
not they might be interested.

■ You don't have time for apologies, for example, 'I won't keep you long',
'Can you spare me a few minutes', 'I'm sorry to take up your time'
(you are inviting your target to say 'No!').

■ Control the conversation but don't dominate.

■ Listen and concentrate – focus all your energy on the conversation.
When people talk they tell you things – listen, and ask questions – get
them to do the talking.

■ Calls are more likely to be successful when:
   ■ *You have selected the right person to contact;*
   ■ *You can link your background to their possible needs;*
   ■ *You have developed some ideas as to the possible role you could
   play in their company and the benefits you bring.*

11. Application forms

Some organisations, particularly in the public sector, do not accept CVs. Instead you are required to submit an application form. The recession has hit the public sector particularly hard, with 15% of local authorities planning to make job cuts in 2009, according to the Local Government Association. But that still leaves 85 per cent who are not planning redundancies. So it is well worth you including public sector vacancies on your target list; and consequently understanding how to best fill in application forms.

The frustrating thing about application forms is that each one has to be written from scratch. Unlike a CV you cannot use a template that you adapt for each application unless you are able to complete your application form electronically. In those cases you can cut and paste a lot of the information from your CV template. More positively, the questions that are asked on an application form tell you a lot about what the organisation is looking for. By paying careful attention to these, you should be able to submit more focused, targeted applications.

All application forms will ask for the same basic information – your personal details, career history and so on. Because they appear in a box on a form there is often a temptation to provide a basic, factual answer, without going into too much detail, in much the same way as you might if you are if you are filling in an application for a passport or bank account. Make sure you resist this. Your application form is every bit as much a sales document as your CV; each and every question that you answer has to communicate your strengths effectively and compellingly. So although you will have to enter your career history in the format demanded by the form, which may well limit the space you have for your answers, you should still ensure that you include the achievements and skills that are relevant to the job, just as you would on your CV.

In addition to the basic information a good application form will ask you questions about why you are applying for this particular job and what relevant experience you have. Treat this as an opportunity; it is not one that you get with a CV-based application. When sending a CV the only opportunity that you get to match yourself in writing to the job is in the covering letter, which is necessarily short. In an application form however, you should be able to be more expansive, particularly if there is a section that allows you to provide further information. But, unless the form specifically says that you can continue on a separate sheet if necessary, make sure that your answers are contained within the space provided.

Equal opportunities and diversity monitoring

Many public sector application forms contain sections that ask you about your age, sexuality, ethnic group and religion. While this might appear intrusive, and to be in conflict with equal opportunities legislation, in fact it is quite legitimate and often required for statutory processes. The application form should make clear that the information is only required for monitoring purposes, that it will be retained by the human resources department and will not be shown to anyone involved in the recruitment process.

Even though it is quite safe to provide this information, if you have been the victim of discrimination in the past you may feel uncomfortable answering these questions. But there is very little you can do about it and in fact if you do get a public sector job you are likely to be asked similar questions every time you enrol on a training course or apply for a promotion. If you really do feel uncomfortable in disclosing personal information, the public sector is probably not the place for you to form a career.

Key points to note about an application form:

■ Follow all the instructions;

■ Answer all the questions fully and concisely;

■ If you are writing rather than typing your answers, make sure your handwriting is legible;

■ Highlight your achievements when describing your previous jobs;

■ Sell yourself strongly as you would on your CV, but remember not to write too much, people can get bored with reading;

■ Complete the sections on diversity and equal opportunities in full;

■ Ensure that you submit your application form on time.

On pages 123–130 is a fairly standard application form used by a large local authority.

Application for Employment

It is important that you read the guidance notes before completing this application form. Please fully complete this form using type or black ink.

A curriculum vitae is not an acceptable form of application unless stated otherwise.

Applications received after the closing date will not normally be considered.

	FOR OFFICE USE ONLY
	Job Title:
	Ref No:
	Closing Date:

The information you supply on this form will be treated in confidence.

Personal details

Last name: _____ First name(s): _____

Address: _____

_____

_____ Post code: _____

Home telephone: _____ Daytime telephone: _____

Mobile telephone: _____

National Insurance No: _____

Email address: _____

Are you applying for a job share? Yes: ☐ No: ☐

Do you have a job share partner? Yes: ☐ No: ☐

Are you able to take up employment in the UK with no current immigration restrictions? Yes: ☐ No: ☐

If you are successful you must provide evidence of the above details prior to your appointment.

1

Current or most recent employment/voluntary work

Employer:

Job Title:

Address:

Post code:

Current/last salary:　　　　　　Grade:　　　　Benefits:

Date commenced:　　　　　　Date of leaving:

Reason for leaving:

Period of notice:

Brief description of main duties/responsibilities: Please continue on a separate sheet if necessary.

Previous employment or work experience record

Please provide full details of all your previous paid and unpaid employment in date order since leaving full-time education, explaining any breaks. Please continue on a separate sheet if necessary. Please refer to guidance notes for further details.

Employer's name and address	From	To	Job Title	Reason for leaving

2

Education, training and qualifications

Starting with the most recent, please give details of educational qualifications you have obtained from School, College, University etc. Shortlisted candidates will be required to provide proof of qualifications obtained. You will be expected to provide evidence of all qualifications listed. Please continue on a separate sheet if necessary.

Name of School, College or University	Qualification	Date taken/ to be taken	Grade

Membership of professional bodies (including General Teaching Council)/professional qualifications

Name of body	Qualification class/ grade of membership	Was membership gained by examination?	Date obtained

3

Further information on knowledge, skills, abilities and experience

Please explain how your experience, knowledge and skills meet the selection criteria in the person specification. **Attach additional sheets if necessary and please address the items in the person specification in the order given.** You can refer to experience and knowledge gained from voluntary work, leisure interests and any other activities which are relevant to this position. Do not attach a CV as it will not be considered. Please continue on a separate sheet if necessary. Please refer to the guidance notes.

Driving Licence details

The enclosed post details will state whether a driving licence is required for the post.

Do you hold a full, clean, current driving licence which enables you to drive in the UK?

Yes: ☐   No: ☐

If yes, please state the type of licence:

If you are successful you will be required to provide evidence of the licence prior to your appointment.

4

References

Please give the names and addresses of two people who can provide an assessment of your suitability for this job. If you are currently employed, or have been employed, you are asked to give your current or most recent employer and another employer. If at School or College, please give the name of your teacher or lecturer, or the name of a person whom we can contact in order to obtain a reference. For some posts, references will be required before the interview. Please refer to the guidance notes.

Reference 1

Name:

Job Title:

Work relationship:

Organisation:

Address:

Post code:

Telephone:

Email:

May we approach them at this stage?

Yes: ☐   No: ☐

Reference 2

Name:

Job Title:

Work relationship:

Organisation:

Address:

Post code:

Telephone:

Email:

May we approach them at this stage?

Yes: ☐   No: ☐

Conflicts of Interest

Relatives/other interests

Are you related to, or do you have a close personal relationship with, a Member (Councillor) or employee of the Council?

Yes: ☐   No: ☐

If yes, please specify:

Name: Position:

Relationship:

Any candidate who directly or indirectly canvasses a Councillor or senior officer of the Council will be disqualified.

If appointed, do you have any interests, carry out any work or hold any appointments that may conflict with this Council's employment?

Yes: ☐   No: ☐

If yes, please detail on a separate sheet.

5

Declarations

Rehabilitation of Offenders Act

If the post for which you have applied for is exempted from the provisions of the Rehabilitation of Offenders Act 1974 (Exceptions) Order 1975 (sl 1975 No.1023) as amended by the Amendment Orders 1986 (sl 1986 Nos 1249 & 2268); you are required to provide **full** details of **all** convictions, cautions and bind overs including those regarded as spent under the ROA, and any pending prosecutions. This would be any post that involves working with and/or access to children or vulnerable adults.

If the post for which you have applied involves substantial opportunity for access to children and/or vulnerable adults the council is entitled, under arrangements for the protection of children or vulnerable adults, to check with the criminal records bureau about the existence and content of any criminal record. CRB checks will only be made about the successful applicant.

Failure to declare a conviction, caution, bind over or a pending prosecution, may disqualify you from appointment or may result in summary dismissal. **However a criminal conviction spent or unspent will not automatically exclude you from employment from the council.**

Do you have a Criminal Conviction(s) or police caution(s), spent or otherwise?   Yes: ☐   No: ☐

If yes, please provide details including dates:

If you answer yes and you are successfully appointed, you will be expected to provide Human Resources with full details of the conviction(s) or offences(s) and make a Criminal Records Bureau Disclosure application.

Further information will be provided to you if the council makes an offer of employment. Please refer to the guidance notes

Data Protection Act 1998

Under the Data Protection Act 1998, the Council reserves the right to collect, store and process personal data about applicants in so far as it is relevant to your application. This also applies during employment and for six years thereafter. This includes processing sensitive data for the purposes of monitoring the Council's equality and diversity policy.

Declaration Statement

Statement to be signed by the applicant

The Council is committed to an anti-fraud culture and participates in statutory anti-fraud initiatives.

I acknowledge that the Council is under a duty to protect the public funds it administers and to this end I agree it may use information provided on this form for the prevention and detection of crime and it may share this information with other bodies solely for these purposes.

I have read, and, if appointed, am prepared to accept, the conditions set out in the conditions of employment and job description.

I confirm that to the best of my knowledge, the information in this application form is true and correct and gives a fair representation of my skills and work experience. I understand that giving false or misleading statements or withholding information may result in disciplinary action including dismissal from the Council or withdrawal of an offer of employment,

I hereby give consent to the collection, storage and processing of my personal data.

Please note: If you are returning this form by e-mail, you will be asked to sign your application upon being called for interview. Candidates selected for interview will normally be notified within three weeks of the closing date.

Signed: _____   Date: _____

6

Equal Opportunities & Diversity Monitoring

In order that we can effectively monitor recruitment, it is a requirement that you complete this section which will then be separated from the application form for shortlisting.

Name:

Job Ref:

Post Title:

Age range:

16 to 19 ☐   20 to 29 ☐   30 to 39 ☐   40 to 49 ☐   50 to 59 ☐   60 to 65 and over ☐

Gender:

Male ☐   Female ☐   ☐

Sexuality:

Bisexual ☐   Heterosexual ☐   Gay ☐   Lesbian ☐   Prefer not to say ☐

Ethnicity:

Asian or Asian British ☐

Bangladeshi ☐

Indian ☐

Pakistani ☐

Other Asian background
(please state)

Mixed

White and Asian ☐

White and Black African ☐

White and Black Caribbean ☐

Other Mixed background
(please state)

Chinese or other Ethnic Group

Chinese ☐

Filipino ☐

Vietnamese ☐

Other Ethnic Group
(please state)

Black or Black British ☐

Caribbean ☐

African:

Eritrean ☐

Ghanaian ☐

Nigerian ☐

Somali ☐

Other African background
(please state)

Other Black background
(please state)

White

British ☐

Greek/Greek Cypriot ☐

Irish ☐

Kurdish ☐

Turkish/Turkish Cypriot ☐

Other White background
(please state)

7

Religion or Belief:

Buddhist	☐	Pagan	☐
Christian	☐	Rastafarian	☐
Hindu	☐	Sikh	☐
Jewish	☐	No religion or belief	☐
Muslim	☐	Prefer not to say	☐

Other religion or belief (Please state)

_____

Disability:

Do you consider yourself to have an impairment or be disabled?

Yes: ☐   No: ☐

If yes:

Are you blind or do you have a visual impairment? ☐

Do you have learning difficulties? ☐

Are you a person with experience of mental health distress? ☐

Do you use a hearing aid or communicate using BSL? ☐

Do you use a walking stick or a wheelchair? ☐

Do you have any other impairment (e.g. diabetes, epilepsy, Multiple Sclerosis, back problem etc. – please state)?

_____

Please explain any special assistance you may need for the interview.

_____

Health

Please state the number of days you have been absent
from work due to sickness in the past 24 months: _____

How many periods of absence does this represent? _____

Please note, a successful candidate will be required to complete a medical questionnaire and may be asked to attend for a medical examination.

Advertising:

How did you find out about this vacancy?

_____

(if from advert, please state publication and date)

_____

Employment Status:

Are you currently unemployed?   Yes: ☐   No: ☐

If yes, how long have you been unemployed? From:

_____

8

12. Interviewing

Getting an interview

Being invited to interview is a major achievement. You would normally expect about one in ten of your job applications to lead to an interview. Once you get to interview you are rarely more than two or three steps away from a job offer. So take your interviews seriously and prepare well.

The purpose of the interview

In theory, the interview is a two way process. On one hand you are trying to persuade the employer that you have the right attributes and capabilities for the role, and they are trying to assess your fit within the company. On the other hand, they are trying to persuade you that you will benefit from taking on the role and you are trying to assess whether you really want it. At least that's the theory. In practice however, most employers walk into an interview room assuming that it is a one way process – they will decide whether to offer you a job and you will be grateful if they do. Most interview candidates see it the same way.

Whether or not you do is up to you; but I would urge you to see yourself as a buyer as much as a seller. You are looking for alignment between what you have to offer and what the employer needs in terms of doing the job, as well as between what you want and what the employer offers in terms of your career development.

After the interview both sides go away to review what took place and to decide whether they want to take the relationship further.

Different types of interview
Telephone interviews

This is most usually used for screening purposes, to decide if you should be invited for a more formal interview. Tone of voice is important on the phone; apart from the content of your answers it is the only thing which enables an interviewer to make a judgement as to your character. Speak clearly, confidently and audibly; as if you were addressing a meeting.

One to one interviews

This is usually conducted by the department head or line manager in question, or someone from human resources. Again it may be a screening interview, to decide whether to invite you to meet the full selection panel.

Panel interviews

Here, two or more people will be present, but rarely more than four. Usually each will be assigned a particular task in terms of what they are looking for from the candidate. Make sure that you get all their names and that you make frequent eye contact with all of them. It is easy to spend the whole interview looking at just one person – don't do it!

Assessment centres

These events tend to include not only interviews but also the opportunity to demonstrate your capability, for example by doing some kind of presentation, and often psychometric or competency tests.

Background research

You will already have submitted your job application and you should have done copious research into the company already. But now it is time to do more! Find out as much as you can about the company. Go to its website and download as much as you can. If it is a large company you should find press releases, annual reports, organisational charts and much more.

If it is a small company the amount of information on the website may be limited, but you may be able to obtain more from Companies House (www.companieshouse.gov.uk) or from a corporate research website.

Try to be as clear as you can about the company's structure, key players, culture, markets, mission and philosophy. Don't just look for key facts and figures, try to understand what's going on. For example, how committed are the workforce to the company? Is it just a job to most of them or do they see themselves as sharing in the success of the company? And how committed is the company to investing in the welfare and personal development of its staff?

In particular, try to be as clear as you can about how the recession is affecting the company. There is no point in you enthusing about being a part of the company's future growth if the company is struggling and all their current activities are focused on survival.

Think of some relevant questions to ask about the company and the team you will be working with. The more informed you are, and the more interest you show, the greater your chances of success. But be careful not to come across too strong; you mustn't appear to have such strong opinions or to be so resolute about the company's options that you come across as a threat to the people interviewing you.

Be clear about how what you offer, in terms of skills and experience, matches what they want. Know what you bring to the company and what you can do to help the company move forward successfully.

First impressions
First impressions are hugely important in defining the way other people relate to us. We make lasting judgements about people within the first

two minutes of meeting them, and those judgements are made on the following basis:

- 55% to do with appearance;
- 38% to do with behaviour;
- 7% to do with what the person actually says.

In other words, by far the most important thing you can do if you want to make a good impression is to 'look the part'. Let's look at each of these three judgements in turn.

Appearance

If you know how people generally dress for the organisation, aim to dress at least as formally for your interview. If in doubt, standard business wear is safest. Be understated: minimal jewellery, dark colours, no loud ties. Even in companies where casual dress is the norm, you should aim to be smart casual, not shabby.

Make sure your hair is neat and clean. Get a trim if need be. Facial hair should be trimmed also. If you're a man go easy on hair preparations and if you're a woman keep your make-up understated.

Don't drink coffee or eat strongly flavoured foods immediately before the interview. However, don't be hungry; eat a banana an hour before the meeting. If you smoke, eat a few mints.

Aim to arrive five to ten minutes before the appointment. Use the time waiting in reception to get a feel for the place. Don't settle down; stay alert and be ready for your host – you don't want to leave them with their hand ready to be shaken while you are folding a newspaper and trying to emerge from a soft, low seat at the same time.

Nervous? Hold a handkerchief to avoid proffering a clammy hand.

Body language

Body language is the other critical aspect in making a positive impression. Your handshake is the only element of physical contact you will have. Don't give a weak handshake even if your host does. When you take the person's hand you should hold it with a bit of a squeeze, but not hard, and accompany it with direct eye contact. As your host introduces herself, repeat her name with a greeting like, "Pleased to meet you Ms Brown", and smile. This simple acknowledgement has a large impact.

Make use of eye contact regularly, but don't stare – keep it warm and natural. Too little means you feel too dominated or are disinterested. Too much is threatening. Face your interviewer directly; sit with an open, relaxed pose. Try to mirror the interviewer's posture as closely as possible – the evidence is that this helps to build rapport. Try not to bunch yourself up – give your lungs space to work properly. Use your hands as part of your communication, but don't force yourself to do anything. It's much more important that you should be focused and natural.

It is often the case that the interviewer will be as nervous, if not more so, than the candidate. After all, they have a big responsibility resting on their shoulders. If they make the wrong appointment, they may get blamed for it. Remember that an interview is a two way process; try to make the interviewer feel at ease by leaning slightly into them, use eye contact and smile.

The discussion

You will be asked different types of questions. Mostly the interview will cover your work history and why you are suited to the job. You may get asked about your education, hobbies and interests. This is generally part of the warm up and is meant to create rapport. If you have any relevant non-work experience you may also be questioned about that.

The golden rules for answering questions are:

- Be honest, do not attempt to give the answer you think the questioner wants to hear – the best answer is the one you believe to be right.

- Listen and make sure you understand the question.

- Keep your answers full but concise – don't talk for too long.

- Shape your answer by taking into consideration the needs and expectations of the company that is interviewing you.

- Don't be afraid of silences. If you feel you have answered the question and the interviewer remains silent, ask if there is anything they would like further detail on. Silence is sometimes used as a way of making you feel uncomfortable and causing you to say more than you intended. Resist it, check that you have said all that you wanted to say, and if so wait for the interviewer to resume.

Competency based interviewing is now the most recognised type of questioning. It works on the principle that past performance is an indicator of future potential. This is why it is highly likely that you will be asked to give examples of past work, particularly successes.

If you are asked a question that you find tricky, try to use the following technique. We call it the *STAR* technique. The word *STAR* alludes to the four parts of your ideal answer: *Situation, Task, Action, Result*: use it to describe something that you did which answers the question.

- *Situation* – outline the situation that you were facing;
- *Task* – What did you need, or were expected, to do?;
- *Action* – How did you deal with the problem?;
- *Result* – What was the outcome?

Practice some answers before the interview, using the *STAR* technique. You will soon see why it is a useful tool.

Listening and telling

Listening is different from hearing. Listening is done as much with the eyes as the ears. What is the meaning behind the question? Consider the intonation of the questioner. How is the questioner saying things? Look attentive. Look as if you are concentrating.

If you are unsure about what the person is asking, paraphrase it back as a check or simply say: *"I'm not sure what you mean by that, would you please explain?"* Don't be afraid about looking a fool by doing this; you'll only look foolish if you interpret the question incorrectly and fly off into an irrelevant answer.

Telling is different from answering. Of course you must always answer the questions but it is entirely up to you how you answer. It is up to you to communicate the messages that are going to impress. Listen for opportunities to get your messages across in your answer.

A good interviewer will give you plenty of opportunity to get your message across by asking you open questions. These are questions that give you the opportunity to expand, rather than just answer yes or no. But if you are facing an interviewer who does not understand about open questions, or chooses not to use them, you must simply take the opportunity when it comes. If you feel you have had very little chance to get your messages across during the interview, ask at the end if you can add a few comments .

If you are doing this, don't insult the interviewer by insinuating that they have not given you a chance; just say that there are one or two things you feel may be of interest to them. Make sure your messages are concise and absolutely relevant. This is a very good opportunity to give an example of something you have done in the past which is relevant but did not come up during the interview.

Feedback and follow up

Don't be surprised if you are invited back for a further interview, many companies now conduct second or third interviews as a matter of course. These could be with more, less, or equally senior people to those already met. Be sure to know who you are seeing and the purpose of the meeting. Do these people have more or less influence in the decision to recruit? Is it confirmation of a decision already taken to offer the job? Maybe you have been invited back to undertake tests that will help identify the particular strengths you will bring, and areas that you will need to develop. Whatever the reason, be prepared to approach the meeting in the appropriate way.

Avoid talking about money as far as possible. Certainly, don't raise this matter. This should be covered indirectly but many employers use the opportunity to take advantage of their position of power to raise the matter.

The way they might do so is to ask you what salary you are looking for. Be as non-committal as you can. The employer should know your worth and what they are prepared to pay. Explain that you are looking for a salary that reflects your value and explain any qualifying factors (economic situation, industry norms, effect of making a career change, location, etc.) Ask what budget they had in mind. The best thing is to be firm and suggest that they should make you an offer to consider. Don't be pressured. Stand your ground. Remember, this is a negotiation.

If you don't get to take things further, you are entitled to know why. It is important to know why you failed in order to evaluate how realistic you are being in your job search. Try to speak to the interviewer if you can, if not insist on having written feedback.

You want to know:
- If you had the right experience and if not, where the gaps were;
- If you answered the questions well;
- If you had the right characteristics to fit into the team or organisation;
- If you appeared interested enough;
- If you failed because you didn't reach the required standard, or if other candidates were better qualified or experienced.

Critically, you should ask for advice that will help you to perform better in a similar situation in the future.

Typical questions

It is impossible to predict what will be asked in an interview but the following seem to come up quite regularly. Preparing for these questions, which cover most angles, is likely to ensure you are prepared for most things you may be asked. Remember the golden rules.

- Always be honest and open;

- Don't be afraid to ask the interviewer to rephrase a question if you don't understand it;

- Answer the question and don't waffle;

- Shape your answer to the company that is interviewing you. This is why research is so valuable;

■ Take time to think about the answer if you need to and don't be afraid of silences. If you feel you have answered the question and the interviewer remains silent while looking engaged, wait a few seconds and ask if that answered the question sufficiently. If it did not, ask if there is anything they would like further detail on.

Question
Tell me about yourself.

Why it is asked
This is a hard question although it is often meant to be a gentle opener. It's hard because it is too open. It is intended to give the interviewer an overview of the candidate.

How to answer
Don't give your life story. Stick to what is relevant, i.e. your career. Give an account of your work life, focusing only on what is relevant to the role for which you are applying, gradually giving more detail as you come up to the present day. Finish off with a short statement about your life outside work to show you are a balanced individual.

Question
What do you see as your key strengths?

Why it is asked
As with all open questions, the interviewer is expecting you to talk at some length rather than with a handful of words that may answer the question in an efficient way.

How to answer
Again, think about the organisation you are trying to impress and relate the answer to their needs. Avoid stock answers like 'good communicator',

'people person', 'hard working' – these are minimum requirements expected of any employee and not strengths. Give examples to illustrate your answers. Try to use the *STAR* method if you are describing a complicated example but ideally stick to fairly straightforward ones.

Question
What are your weaknesses? Or, What are the areas you would most like to improve?

Why it is asked
This question aims to explore your self-awareness and integrity. It is not intended to undo you, but it can help the questioner to assess if your development needs can be addressed by the organisation and if you are likely to struggle in the role.

How to answer
Don't try to be too clever by disguising a strength as a weakness and leaving it at that. An example might be, "I work very long hours and never see my family". A good interviewer will probe you on this to see why you believe it to be a weakness. Be careful not to admit to a weakness that might prejudice your ability to carry out the role.

You might also think about weaknesses that you have but which you have developed strategies to deal with. An example might be time management, where you make diligent use of technology to ensure you keep on top of projects or appointments. You might also choose to describe what you like least in work, as opposed to what you consider to be a weakness. This is a way of telling the interviewer about what you are inclined to avoid doing rather than what you cannot do. Again, showing that you are aware of this and that you know how to handle it demonstrates maturity.

Question
Is there anything you would have preferred to have done differently in your career?

Why it is asked
Again looking for weaknesses, you are being asked to identify examples of poor performance.

How to answer
Give an example, not too recent, preferably of something that didn't go well but that can be put down to lack of experience (rather than poor skills or bad judgement). This is an opportunity to show how you can learn from your mistakes.

Question
Can you give me an example of (any work experience)?

Why it is asked
The classic competency question, as mentioned earlier, is asked because it is recognised that past experience is a good indicator of future performance.

How to answer
Have a portfolio of examples covering your career history and experience (i.e. not just most recent roles, and making sure you cover the different types of activity you have been involved with). Commit these to memory in the *STAR* format and be ready to select from them as appropriate.

Question
Why are you leaving/did you leave your current/last job?

Why it is asked

If you have been made redundant, don't worry; say so. There is no stigma attached to this nowadays. However, this question is also asking you to identify what you are looking for from a job that your current/last employer could not provide.

How to answer

Never badmouth your current employer! Don't even imply personality clashes. This is all about what you want to achieve and your judgement about how best to do it.

If you have been made redundant explain the circumstances succinctly. Show that any bitterness no longer exists and that you are looking at it as an opportunity to move your career forward.

Question

I'm concerned that you are over-qualified for this role. How do you react to that?

Why it is asked

The interviewer is worried that the role lacks sufficient challenge for you and that you may leave sooner than expected.

How to answer

If you feel the role will be good for your long-term career aims, and that by performing well you would hope for promotion then say so, but don't give an answer that may make the questioner feel threatened. If you have a work–life balance issue or want to get back to 'hands on' work after a period in management then say so. These are legitimate reasons for taking what most might consider a 'smaller' job than you previously held.

Do not say that you really need any job and can't find one at the right level, or that you are prepared to take a salary cut in order to get into work. Nobody will wish to employ you on this basis, not least because you are likely to continue looking for another more suitable position from the start.

Question
Do you work well under pressure?

Why it is asked
A closed question, easy to answer but difficult to answer well.

How to answer
Of course you work well under pressure, who would ever admit that they don't? To stand out from the crowd with this question give one or two clear examples. Assuming that it is normal to work under pressure in this company, you may also wish to talk about what you consider to be an acceptable level of pressure and ask what the interviewer means by it. There are different types of pressure: time demands, responsibility without authority, lack of support, etc. It would help to define what types of pressure you cope best with.

Question
What would you do if a talented employee was not pulling their weight and this was causing friction within the team?

Why it is asked
Questions like this are asked to see how the candidate would handle a conflict between two equally important values. In this case disciplining a talented employee whom you value versus the morale of the wider team. There are a number of ways in which you might be asked to describe a hypothetical scenario, this is just one. Another might be to look at how you would deal with a situation where you disagreed with

your boss on a work related issue, or how you would handle a client that was making unreasonable demands.

How to answer
You need to show maturity of thought when answering such questions. Take your time to think through the conflict being presented and listen to your own sense of integrity before giving your answer. To spend a few seconds thinking before answering would be appropriate, but not too long, you don't want the interviewer to feel bored or uncomfortable and you also need to show that you can think on your feet.

It's a good idea to draw upon your own experience whenever possible by giving examples of how you have managed a similar situation in the past.

Question
What is your management style?

Why it is asked
This question has no right or wrong answer. The interviewer will be looking for a well thought out argument that you can defend, rationally and articulately. It can also be used to see if your management style fits into the corporate culture.

How to answer
The best answer here is to show that you are a flexible manager who is able to adapt to different situations as the need arises. However, you ought to explain the style that comes most naturally to you and say why it works for you.

Question
What has been the toughest part of your job in the past year or so?

Why it is asked

This question is purposely asked in a negative frame to see if you will fall in the trap of equating tough with weakness.

How to answer

Think challenging, not weakness. Give an example of something that was hard but which gave you satisfaction once you had completed it successfully.

Question

What do you see as the main task of a (role you are applying for)?

Why it is asked

You are asked this so the interviewer can gauge how well you have prepared for the interview.

How to answer

Don't play back the job description. This best way to answer this is to show that you have thought about how you might handle the issues that are likely to arise by referring to your particular skills.

Question

I'm concerned that you do not have as much experience as we are expecting for this role.

Why it is asked

Most employers will be comparing you not only against the criteria set out in the job description but also against other candidates, therefore this may be referring to relative weakness. Nevertheless you should assume that you have qualities of interest to the employer to have got to this stage and therefore you have a chance of getting the position.

How to answer

Do your homework and some objective self-assessment to identify shortcomings in your experience. Acknowledge these, perhaps with your thoughts as to the relative importance of each to the post, and then move on to describe the compensating factors that you feel will enable you to do a good job while you are developing the other required capabilities.

Question

Where do you see yourself in five years time?

Why it is asked

This may be asked about any length of time but rarely more than five years as this is too far away for most people to plan in much detail; there are too many variables. A shorter time span than three years is probably looking to see how quickly you would expect promotion, while three to five years is asking about what you see as your next role after this.

How to answer

Focus on where you see your career going over the medium term and explain how you see this role fitting into the game plan. Try not to give specific timings about when you think things are likely to happen. This is an opportunity to talk about the career development support you will be looking for. It would also go down well if you expressed how you are looking for a company that rewards good performance with promotion opportunities.

Question

Why might you not accept this position if it were offered to you?

Why it is asked

A tricky question testing integrity. It's looking for you to expand on exactly what you are looking for in your next job. If asked early on in the interview, the objective may be to put you on the back foot to see how you cope under pressure. If asked towards the end, it is more of a winding down question. In this situation they may have decided they would like to take things further and are just making sure about things.

How to answer

Again, honesty is key. You should be clear in your own mind about what you are expecting in terms of the company culture, level of autonomy, prospects, etc. You might also wish to talk about the package being appropriate for the level of responsibility, and your expectations.

Question

Who would you like to see winning Big Brother?

Why it is asked

Question like this, often asked unexpectedly, are known as 'killer questions' and are popular with some interviewers these days. The idea is to see how mature your social skills are by testing your ability to converse, and to check how in touch with the wider culture you are.

How to answer

Your answer, or opinion is irrelevant. The key is to give an argued opinion, and a fairly strong one is better than a passive one. What do you think about Big Brother, or this type of TV in general? Show that you can have a conversation with a stranger on any subject.

13. The job offer

We may be in a recession but you have just been offered a job! Now you need to know that what you are being offered is in line with your expectations and that the company values you appropriately. It is natural in a hirer's job market for employers to try to get themselves a bargain when recruiting new staff. Don't fall for it! Even in a recession you should never undervalue yourself; something better could come along at any moment.

Be clear about what you want from the job.

It is not just about salary. Your next job has got to take you forward in the way you want. Review your career plan; will taking this job allow you to progress in the way you want? Will it improve your CV, and will it look good in three years time when you start thinking about your next role?

What about the people? Do you think you can work with them? Who will you be reporting to, what is their management style and will you have as much independence or team work as you need? Is the culture of the firm to your liking? Did you feel comfortable when you went for interview? What about the package? Is it as good as you wanted or can you improve on it? There is always an option to negotiate, don't be intimidated into accepting the first thing they offer you?

Finally, what about security? How is the company doing in the recession? Does it have a future or are they recruiting in a last-ditch effort to save the business before it goes under? Will you be part of that future? These questions are not usually necessary, but right now they are essential.

Job essentials

A good way to evaluate whether the job you have been offered will be right for you is to prepare a 'job essentials list' in advance. Then, when you are offered a job you can go to this list and see how well it matches your needs. A job essentials list will contain some of the following. You don't need to pick them all, just select the ones that you feel are essential:

Location
- How far are you prepared to travel (time or distance)?

- What are your location needs (e.g. working outdoors, not working in the country, working in a town centre)?

The company
- What is the ideal size and structure?

- What is the culture?

- What are the company's values?

- What demands will working for the company make on your family or private life?

- What will your boss/line manager be like? What is their working and management style?

Working conditions
- What sort of space do you want to work in (e.g workshop, open plan office, private office, retail floor)?

- What facilities should there be (e.g crèche, pool room, canteen, sports facilities)?

The role
- What tasks would your ideal role require you to perform?

- What would you see as the ideal consequences of the work you do?

- What is your ideal work–life balance?

- What is your ideal team/solo working balance?

- What are the prospects for career advancement, promotion, personal development?

- What training opportunities do you want?

The package
- What salary do you expect?

- What pension package do you expect?

- What bonus and share options do you expect?

- What benefits (health and life insurance, car, expense account, club membership) do you expect?

Once you have written your list of job essentials you can draw up a chart like this. The match column is your assessment of how the job offer compares with your ideal. If the final match total is 75% or above, it is likely that this is the right job for you.

Job essential	My ideal	This job offers	Match
Distance from home	30 minutes	45 minutes	75%
Location	Rural outlook	Suburban office	60%
Company Values	Good commitment to social responsibility	Won an award in 2006 for their environmental projects	120%
Salary	£60K	£70K	110%
Pension	Final salary scheme	8% contribution to personal pension fund.	80%
		Match total (average of percentages)	**89%**

Can't get or don't want a job?

14. What are you going to do now?

You are out of work, we are in the middle of a recession, jobs are in short supply and you decide this moment presents the opportunity that you have been waiting for to change your life. You have never really enjoyed working, always felt that there is something better out there for you and now is the time to do something about it. You don't know what it is you want, but the one thing you do know is that you never want to work for someone else again. You want to be your own boss.

Great. The idea that good career consultants place above all others is that everyone is entitled to a working life that stimulates, satisfies and fulfils them. In your case this means creating a working life for yourself that is self-directed; in which what you do does not depend on the fortunes of the third party that you work for, nor on what a manager or boss tells you to do.

So if you are not going to work for someone else, what are you going to do? Unless you intend to live on benefits, become a gambler or turn to crime, then the only remaining option you have is to work for yourself. And if self employment is the way you want to go, then you have two routes to choose from. You can either start your own business, which includes setting up on your own if you are a professional, such as a lawyer or accountant, or you can do a number of different things, either short term or permanent, for different employers. The latter category includes both consultancy and portfolio careers.

Before looking at the relative merits of each of these routes, and what you need to do to get started, you'll probably find it useful to work through the following exercises, which will give you a better idea of how well suited you are to self employment. There are no right or wrong answers to these questions, making the decision to go self employed is just one of many decisions that you will have to take by yourself. So you will just have to be honest with yourself, answer the questions as best you can and make a decision based on your responses.

Do you have the right blend of personal qualities for self-employment?

Below is a list of qualities. In the second column, tick each quality you feel you possess. It's not always easy to answer these questions yourself, so talk to your friends, family and people you know. Remember, it is very important to be honest with yourself. Don't tell yourself what you want to believe; this is the surest way to go wrong

Think back over your life and think of examples that will convince someone that you have the quality required. You may not be able to give an example for everything. If that's the case, just put 'no example' in the space provided.

Quality	Tick	Example
Determination, resilience, persistence Are you convinced that you can succeed against the odds? Are you the sort of person who bounces back from a setback? Is your motto 'if at first you don't succeed, try, try, try again'?		
Intuition Is your gut feeling usually right? Do you generally make good decisions with very little information?		
Toughness Are you willing to make unpopular decisions? Are you prepared to be tough in difficult circumstances? Are you ready to argue your corner with clients, or to fire someone if need be, for example?		
Drive Success rarely comes overnight. Are you driven, prepared to succeed against the odds, or are you likely to back down if things don't work out the way you planned?		
Self-confidence Do you believe you have the capabilities and skills to make a success of self employment? Do you feel you have something to offer that sets you apart from most other people in the market?		
Decision-making ability Are you able to make decisions quickly if needed, or do you tend to put off decision making until the last minute, or until the issue goes away?		
Pragmatism Are you prepared to forgo your principles if it would be in your best interests? Can you let go of something that you feel strongly about?		

Quality	Tick	Example
Physical stamina Are you prepared to work late into the night, and at weekends, if necessary? Are you prepared to give up your other interests and hobbies from time to time?		
Resourcefulness Are you able to find solutions to problems quickly? Do you know how and where to access the resources needed to solve problems? Do you tackle problems head on or do you tend to avoid problems?		
Risk taking Are you comfortable with periods of little or no income? Are you willing to risk income or assets in order to support your business? Can you cope without job security?		
Creativity Are you imaginative and full of ideas? Are you open minded to new opportunities and ideas?		
Taking responsibility Do you accept your mistakes and learn from them? Do you look to see how you can avoid similar mistakes in the future, or do you try to find an excuse for your mistakes? How do you react to criticism?		
Flexibility Are you adaptable and able to listen to others? Do you carry on easily if circumstances turn against you or do you freeze when you need to make crucial decisions?		
Organisation Are you well organised and disciplined? Do you set your own agenda and plan for what might happen or react to what's happening around you?		
Status Being self employed means doing many of the jobs you don't want to do. Are you happy to do the boring tasks?		

Obstacles to self-employment

For many people, successful self-employment promises what cannot be achieved by working for someone else. However, self-employment inevitably means making significant changes in your life. Below are a number of issues. Consider how these will be affected should you decide to make the move to self-employment.

Lifestyle

How is self-employment going to affect you in terms of:
Income in the short term?

Time away from home?

Ability to predict where you will be, and when?

Pursuit of outside interests and hobbies?

Time available to spend with your family?

Your own business or a consultancy or portfolio career?

If your answers to these questions have given you the confidence to continue to consider self-employment, the next big question, in fact the most important one, is what will you do? Will you set up your own business or will you find a number of different activities, working for different organisations, which will combine to provide you with the income, security and lifestyle you need?

As a general rule, unless you have a good business idea, and are confident that it will work, you should not start a business. Whatever you do, don't just forge ahead with the first thing that comes into your head – unless you are a savvy and consummate business person that route is bound to fail.

The only time this warning does not apply is when you are considering buying a franchise. In this case you need to do your research well and take the advice of franchise professionals. You should find the British Franchise Association useful.

Starting a business is a major step; it is likely to involve a significant lifestyle change and an upheaval to your finances, at least in the short term. It is not a move that can be undone easily. The list below will give you some idea of the things you need to think about when contemplating starting a business.

Things to consider when starting a business:
The basics

Do you have the idea? Have you researched the market and are you confident your idea will succeed?

The idea

What are the costs of setting up and the barriers to entry (what will prevent others from copying your idea). Do you have particular skills that will give you an advantage in the market?

The knowledge
What do you know about the various aspects of running a business? For example, sales, marketing, product development, financial management, people management, statutory requirements. Are you prepared to learn on the job or would you be better off getting the necessary knowledge by working for someone else; learning from other people's mistakes rather than your own?

Resources
What resources do you need to set up the business, e.g. finance, premises, equipment, customers and suppliers, etc. Do you know how you will get these? Do you know anyone who will be able to help?

Support network
Are the important people in your life behind you? You will need their support. Do you know people who you can go to for advice?

Funding
How long can you survive without an income? How much do you need for working capital?

Risk
What is your attitude to risk? Can you cope with periods of significant financial uncertainty and career insecurity? How will you deal with the inevitable occasion when your bank account is in the red, the payment you have been promised has not materialised and the creditor you have promised to pay is threatening legal action?

Consultancy careers

You may decide that you are not ready to start a business, or that you do not know which business to start, but that you are still determined to work for yourself. In this case you might want to look at a consultancy career or, more probably in the early days, a portfolio career. When we talk about consultancy careers we include anything at all which involves you working on your own and in which clients take advantage of your particular expertise. We are using the word consultancy as a shorthand; otherwise we are just going to get bogged down in terminology.

A consultancy career involves you providing services directly to clients, who are usually, but not always, organisations. Many people begin a consultancy career by working on a freelance basis for their last employer. This is a good arrangement for both sides; the employer already has confidence in you and your abilities, and can pay for work actually done rather than paying a full time salary. You get your new career started relatively easily without having to sell your services cold to people who know nothing about you.

A portfolio career typically contains two or more principal activities that you will divide your working week between. It can be an end in itself, if you want a career that is variable and flexible. Or it can be a short-term opportunity, a particularly good way of maintaining an income while building up a reputation in the area of consultancy in which you want to specialise.

Portfolio activities may include doing some consultancy work in an area where you have a particular expertise, acting as a mentor to a company whose staff do things you know about, managing a particular project, helping out a friend or ex-colleague with their business.

There are no hard and fast rules about what constitutes a consultancy /portfolio career, nor about how many different activities you are likely to undertake. What is probable however is that some, if not all, of your activities will be short term contracts and that you will need to build time into your working week to enable you to look for new contracts as your existing ones begin to expire. In fact you will be faced with the same problem as anyone who sets up a consultancy; you may well find that you spend more time selling the service than carrying it out. Rather than being a consultant you become a sales person.

Employment or self-employment ?

You can see that the decision to work for yourself is a much bigger one than deciding to get another job. It may feel like the best thing to do in a recession, because of the shortage of jobs available, but that is actually a false economy. Recessions pass and the difficult job market will ease. If fundamentally you want the security and regular salary that a permanent job offers, however difficult it may be to get right now, don't sacrifice it for an easy-to-set-up self-employed career that will involve you in financial and possible staff commitments and from which you may not be able to walk away easily.

On the other hand, if deep down you feel that you are meant to be working for yourself and that the recession provides you with an opportunity to do something that you are passionate about; go for it. There is no reason to delay.

Further support

This book will help you to gain an advantage in the tough job market and get back to work much faster than your competitors. But looking for a job is a lonely process, and can be demoralising and unsettling. One of the biggest problems is loss of confidence; all it takes is a few rejections in a short space of time and you begin to feel there is something wrong with you, that you have no chance of getting a job, and so on. While these feelings are natural and understandable, don't take them to heart. Everybody goes through periods like this. It is just tough doing it on your own – and sometimes even tougher when friends and family try to help. They mean well but job hunting is generally not their area of expertise.

Overconfidence can be another pitfall. It is all too easy to write a CV that is too bullish, or to develop an interview style which comes across as too self-assured. The trouble is that you cannot be objective about yourself, you cannot see yourself as others do.

Alternatively, you may be adept at marketing yourself, communicating your strengths and your offer expertly and effectively. But you have no one to communicate it to! You just can't find the jobs to apply for. Your networks are not good enough, and you are just not that adept at research.

These are all good reasons to seek professional assistance with your job search. Thousands of people do it every year; it is as natural as going to a lawyer or accountant for assistance with specialist matters that they know about and you don't. At Career Energy we meet dozens of people every month who want to give their job search that extra edge, and know that objective, professional and expert support will provide it for them.

If you follow the steps outlined in this book you will succeed in your job search. But if you want that little bit extra, or if you are feeling that it is too tough to do it on your own, please get in touch with us. You will find us at *www.careerenergy.co.uk* or you can call *0845 226 1616* or email *info@careerenergy.co.uk*. We have consultants around the country and we are looking forward to your call.

Wishing you every success with your job search – and looking forward to a speedy end to the recession.

The Career Energy Team

Career Energy
5–6 Staple Inn
London
WC1V 7QH
0845 226 1616
www.careerenergy.co.uk
info@careerenergy.co.uk

Index

Note: Page references in *italics* indicate charts and examples.

achievement statements 70, 72–6, 82–3, *84, 86, 88*
achievements:
    and application forms 122
    identifying 39–48
    and job applications 62
    and speculative letters 108
    see also skills
action words 68, 75, *77*, 82, 109
advertisements:
    client-paid 94
    internet 94–5
    menu 92–3, 94
    by recruitment consultants 92–3, 94–5
    responding to *see* applications
Alert Data 105
appearance 134–5
application forms 120–30
    and achievements 122
    and career history 120–1
    example *123–30*
    public sector 121
    targeting 120
applications 58–64
    covering letters 59, 61–2, *63–4*, 121
    CVs 65–89
    and salary history 60
    and self-marketing 38–57, 122
    speculative 36, 102–5, 106–11
    targeting 9–10, 91, 103
assessment centres 132

body language 132, 135
British Franchise Association 159
business, starting 159–60

career consultants 23, 154, 163–4
Career Energy 10, 163–4
career history:
    in application forms 120–1
    in CVs 70, 71–5
    in interviews 142
career plan 149
careers advice 10–11
co-operation 8–9
cold calling 112–19
    advantages 112
    dealing with objections 23, 117–18
    objectives 113
    planning and rehearsing 115
    requesting meeting 23–5, 116
    scripted conversations 113–15
    targeting individuals 24, 112–13
    traps and pitfalls 116–17
companies:
    culture 149, 150
    decision makers 17, 104, 105
    researching 17, 22, 25, 61, 97, 102–5, 106, 139
    security 149
Companies House 133
confidence, loss of 163
consultancy careers 161–2
contacts *see* networking
CV 62, 65–89
    covering letter 59, 61–2, 121
    effective 65–89

fonts and typesizes 68, 82, 83, *85, 87, 89*

length 68, 82, *87, 89*

as marketing document 65–8, 90–1, 96

readability 68–9

and recruitment agencies 93–4, 96, 97

structure 69–76

career history 70, 71–5, *84–5, 86–7, 89;* education and training 78, *85, 87, 89;* interests and hobbies 78, *85, 87, 89;* personal information *85, 87, 89;* professional bodies 79, *85, 87, 89;* profile 69–70; publications *85, 87, 89;* skills and achievements 67, 70, 71–6, 82, 84, *88*

styles 66–8

achievement focused *84–5;* chronological 67; functional 67, *88–9;* industry-specific *68;* responsibilities-focused 67; skills-focused 67, *86–7*

and targeting 59, 61, 82

truthful 66, 76, 82, *85, 87, 89*

updating 65

worksheet *80–1*

decision makers, contacting 16, 17, 104, 112

diversity monitoring 121, 122, *129*

education, in CVs 78, *85, 87, 89*

elevator pitches 27–8

equal opportunities 121, 122, 129

eye contact, at interviews 132, 135

Facebook 29, 31–2, 107

feedback, and interviews 139

fonts and typesizes 68, 82, 83, 85, 87, 89

franchises 159

Gardella, Robert S. 91

Google 107

headhunting 92

hooks, in speculative letters 107–8, *111*

Human Resources departments 20

interests and hobbies 11

in CVs 78, *85, 87, 89*

and self-employment 156, 158

internet advertising 94–5

interviews 131–48

and appearance 134

and body language 132, 135

competency-based 136, 142

dealing with questions 135–8, 139–48

and feedback 139

first impressions 133–5

follow-up 138

mock 96

pre-interview research 132–3

with recruitment consultants 95–6, 97–9

and researching companies 103, 139

and salary discussion 138

silences 136, 140

STAR technique 136–7, 141

types 132

job advertisements:
    analysing 60–1
    by recruitment consultants 92–3
    see also applications
job boards, online 7, 16, 29–36, 94–5
job essentials list 150–1, *152*
job offers 149–52
job searching:
    direct/indirect methods 18
    proactive 14, 16–18
        cold calling 112–19; and
        research 17, 103, 106;
        speculative approaches 102–5,
        106–11; and targeting 9–10, 14,
        16, 82, 91, 103
    reactive 14, 15, 18
    and recession 7–12
job security 149
jobs market 7–8

killer questions, at interviews 148

Lees, John 91
letters:
    with CV 59, 61–2, *63–4*, 121
    length 58
    proofreading 108
    speculative 106–11
lifestyle, and self employment 157–8
LinkedIn 29, 30–1, 33–4, 107–8
listening 117, 119, 137

management style 145, 149
mock interviews 96
Monster 8, 94
motivators 11

networking:
    contact lists 23–4
    online/social 19, 29–35
        disadvantages 29, 32–4; useful
        sites 29–32
    and opportunity lists 35–6
    personal 19–28, 34
        example script 22–3; and
        follow-up 26–7; identification of
        networks 23–4; presentation
        statements 27–8; questions to
        ask 25–6; steps 24–5
    and proactive job searching 16, 91,
        103
    value 8, 15, 19–21

opportunity lists 35–6

panel interviews 132
pensions 151
portfolio careers 161–2
presentation statements 27–8
press advertising 95
proofreading:
    of CVs 82
    of letters 108
public sector 120, 121

recession:
    effects on public sector 120
    and increasing co-operation 8–9
recruitment:
    contingency 92, 93, 95
    search 92
    selection 92, 95
    by word of mouth 106
recruitment consultants 7, 90–101

and advertising 92-3, 94-5
choosing 96-7
fees 92, 93, 95
industry-specific 90-1
interviews with 95-6, 97-9
managing 97-9
record sheets *100-1*
recruitment methods 91-3
and reworking CVs 82, 93-4, 97
sector-specific 95
recruitment process 19, 20
redundancy 143
references 79, 82, 85, 87, 89
research:
    cold calling 112-13
    for interviews 132-3
    and job applications 61, 97, 139
    and job searching 17, 22, 25
    resources 104
    and speculative applications
        101-5, 106
responsibilities, in CV 67, 71-2, 75, 82

salary 60, 85, 87, 89, 138, 151
schools and colleges, and career advice
    10-11
screening interviews 132
selection criteria 59, 60, 62
self-employment 154-62
    and consultancy 161-2
    and franchises 159
    and lifestyle 158
    necessary personal qualities for
        155-8
    obstacles to 158-9
self-marketing 38-57, 122
    and effective CVs 65-8, 90-1, 95

silences in interviews 136, 140
skills 11, 50-2
    audit 49-55
    in CV 67, 70-1, *84*
    everyday 55
    identifying 38-42, 57
    skills focused CVs 67, *86-7*
    transferable 39, 49
    undeveloped 55-6
    see also achievements
spelling, checking 82
STAR technique 136-7, 141
strengths, communicating 10, 25, 28, *84*,
    140-1

targeting
    of applications 91, 103, 120
    of cold calls 112-13
    of CVs 61, 82
    of individuals in company 106-7
    of jobs 9-10, 14, 16
telephone interviews 61, 132
telephoning *see* cold calling
telling and answering, at interviews
    137-8
TotalJobs 94
truth, in CVs 66, 76, 82, 85, *87, 89*

values 11
verbs, action 68, 75, *77*, 82

weaknesses 141-2, 146
work experience, unpaid 16
work-life balance 143, 151
working conditions 150

Xing 32, 34

Index compiled by Meg Davies (Fellow of the Society of Indexers)